EXPENSIV

Peter Mayle was named as Travel
Author of the Year in 1991 by the British Book Awards.
He now lives in the Lubéron with his wife.

Also by Peter Mayle in Pan Books

A Year in Provence
Toujours Provence
Up the Agency

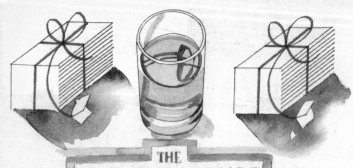

THE
BURLINGTON ARCADE

CAVIAR

THE UNITED STATES OF AMERICA

TEN DOLLARS

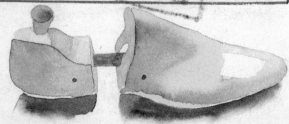

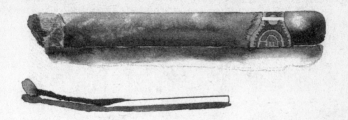

EXPENSIVE
HABITS

Peter Mayle

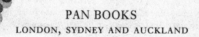

PAN BOOKS
LONDON, SYDNEY AND AUCKLAND

First published in Great Britain 1991 by Sinclair-Stevenson Limited
This edition published 1992 by Pan Books Ltd
a division of Pan Macmillan Publishers Limited
Cavaye Place London SW10 9PG
and Basingstoke

Associated companies throughout the world

ISBN 0 330 32469 1

Acknowledgements: 'A Gentleman's Fetish' was previously published in
Esquire. All other pieces, with the exception of 'The Genuine £1000
Folding Hat' and 'Conjuring with Grapes' first appeared in *GQ*.

1 3 5 7 9 8 6 4 2

A CIP catalogue record for this book is available from
the British Library

Printed in England by Clays Ltd, St Ives plc

For Martin Beiser, whose encouragement was only equalled
by his bravery in the face of my expenses.

Contents

INTRODUCTION

Most of us, I believe, are born with a latent tendency towards extravagance, a lust for more and better which lurks somewhere down in the genes, ready to erupt at the hint of good fortune and the drop of a credit card. What else can explain the the persistent purchase of shoes by a woman who already owns 399 pairs, the acquisition of a second helicopter, a fifth house, another dozen decorator cushions, a drum full of caviare, a methuselah of champagne? Who needs all that? Who buys it? And why?

The spending habits of the rich have intrigued me for years. Above all, I was curious to know if their little luxuries were actually worth the money. Were they paying for something special, or did the real pleasure, the fizz in the veins, come from the giddy feeling of being able to have whatever you want whenever you want it, and to hell with the cost? It was a question that recurred every time I brooded over an irate letter from American Express.

And then one day destiny intervened to help me find the answer. Martin Beiser of *GQ* magazine, a man of consummate faith and infinite expenses, had been told of my scholarly interest in the best that life is reputed to offer, and he was kind enough to give me my marching orders. Go forth, he said, and mingle with the wealthy. Do as they do, providing you obtain clearance from the Accounts Department first, and report back.

It is probably appropriate here to say a word or two about the circumstances in which I normally live. They're modest. I have one house, one small car, one bicycle and four seldom-worn suits. Food and wine, since I'm lucky enough to live in an agricultural area of southern France, are good and inexpensive. My vices are relatively cheap, and I spend more money on books than anything else. I have no wish for a yacht, a racehorse, a butler or even a crocodile attaché case with solid brass fittings and a combination lock, let alone the possessions that really gobble money – a vineyard in Bordeaux, for instance, or a collection of Impressionist art. I can admire and appreciate all these wonderful things, but I don't want to own them. They are, as far as I'm concerned, more trouble than they're worth. They end up owning you.

This was brought home to me one evening a few years ago at the home of a charming couple who suffered from being abnormally rich. One of their guests – it may have been me, now I come to think of it – accidentally nudged the heavy gilt frame of a murky painting in the living room. The alarm went off, and the security service had to be called and reassured and placated before we could sit down to dinner. While we were eating, our hostess spoke about another daily problem, that of the cutlery. It was beautiful old sterling silver, irreplaceable and heavily insured; a priceless heirloom. Unfortunately, the insurance was only valid if the cutlery during its off-duty moments was kept in a safe, and so knives, forks and spoons had to be counted and locked up after every meal.

Well, you may say, these are only minor drawbacks to the otherwise enviable life of bliss that is enjoyed by the congenitally rich. But, after pressing my nose up against the window and watching them in action from time to time, I'm not at all sure that they enjoy themselves as much as we think they do. And why? Because, damn it, something is always *not quite right*.

Expectations tend to increase in direct proportion to the amount of money being spent, and if you're spending a fortune you expect perfection. Alas, life being the badly organised shambles that it so often is, and with so much of it dependent on the behaviour of erratic equipment (servants), perfection is rare. After a while, the rich realise this, and then they start looking for trouble. I've seen them do it. Details that we would consider trivial assume enormous significance: the breakfast egg is inedible because it is marginally underboiled, the silk shirt is unwearable because of a barely visible wrinkle, the chauffeur is insupportable because he's been eating garlic again, the door-man is either insufficiently attentive or over-familiar – the list of maddening blots on the landscape of life just goes on and on. How can you have a nice day if some fool hasn't warmed your socks or ironed your newspaper properly?

I remember a fact-finding mission to a luxury hotel in Venice, a magnificent establishment with an equally magnificent chef. Impossible, I thought, to fail to enjoy dinner in such a place. But I was wrong. Sitting at the next table were four resplendent examples of old money from Milan. They were not happy. The white wine was not chilled exactly to their taste. A finger was lifted, but the waiter took longer than thirty seconds to arrive. Good grief, what is the world coming to? Throughout dinner, I could hear totally unjustified mutterings of discontent. No matter how delicious the food, how splendid the surroundings, things were *not quite right*. And this atmosphere – almost sus-picious, poised for disappointment – pervaded the entire room. There wasn't a jolly millionaire in sight. It was the first and only time I have ever eaten in a subdued Italian restaurant.

After a few experiences like this, the thought of living perma-nently among the rich doesn't appeal to me at all. But I have to say that some of their minor investments – the small conso-lation prizes that they award themselves as they struggle to get through each day – are extremely pleasant, and potentially habit-forming. Once you've tasted caviare, it's hard to contem-plate a tuna salad sandwich with any real gusto.

Perhaps the single most enjoyable part of my researches, which covered a period of about four years, was meeting the artists themselves, the people who provide the luxuries. All of them, from tailors and bootmakers to truffle hunters and champagne blenders, were happy in their work, generous with their time and fascinating about their particular skills. To listen to a knowledgeable enthusiast, whether he's talking about a Panama hat or the delicate business of poaching foie gras in

Sauternes, is a revelation, and I often came away wondering why the price wasn't higher for the talent and patience involved.

In contrast to the pieces devoted to deliberate indulgence, I have included one or two items of involuntary expenditure. None of us can avoid Christmas, tipping, or lawyers, and it seemed to me that any review of the ways in which we are separated from our money should mention them, since they are permanently and expensively with us. So indeed is the Inland Revenue, but the thought of writing about it was too depressing, and any truly candid comments would undoubtedly have led to all my deductions for next year being disallowed by way of revenge.

As we're now going through a period of hard economic times, it may seem inappropriate to present these glimpses of high-level expenditure. But what would life be without the occasional treat? Anyway, as I had to keep telling the Accounts Department, true quality is a bargain.

A
GENTLEMAN'S
FETISH

There are two or three discreet establishments in London that for generations have catered to one of man's lesser known vices. Their names are not advertised, except by word of mouth. Their premises have the hushed atmosphere that discourages loud speech or sudden movement. Conversation is muted and thoughtful, punctuated by occasional subdued creakings. The clients, almost to a man, sit or stand with heads bowed and eyes directed downward, as if reflecting on matters of considerable importance. And indeed they are. These gentlemen, after all, are investing £750 or more in a pair of hand-cut, hand-stitched, hand-built shoes, created solely for the very personal idiosyncrasies of toes and contusions and bony outcroppings that make up the unique gentlemanly foot.

To some men – even those who revel in bespoke suits with cuff buttonholes that really undo, or made-to-measure shirts with single-needle stitching and the snug caress of a hand-turned collar even to some of these satorial gourmets, the thought of walking around on feet cocooned in money somehow smacks of excess, more shameful than a passion for cashmere socks, and something they wouldn't care to admit to their accountants. Their misgivings are usually supported by the same argument: what could possibly justify the difference in price between shoes made by hand and shoes made by machine? Unlike the miracles of disguise that a tailor has to perform in order to camouflage bodily imperfections, the shoemaker's task is simple. Feet are feet.

They're wrong, of course. What they don't understand, and will never understand until enlightened by experience, is the addictive combination of practical virtues and private pleasures enjoyed by the man who has his shoes made by artists.

It all starts with a ritual of initiation, and like any good ritual this one proceeds at a measured pace. You are not here to buy and run. You are committing your feet to posterity, and you must allow at least an hour for your first visit, maybe longer if your requirements are the kind that raise an eyebrow. But that comes later. First you must meet your guide, the man who will escort you through the opening ceremony. In more humdrum establishments, he might be called the fitter or the head salesman. But this shop is one of the last outposts of late Victorian baroque English, and he would probably prefer to think of himself as the purveyor.

He will greet you courteously, but his eyes will not be able to resist flickering downwards for a brief assessment of your shoes. Nothing will be said, but you will be conscious, perhaps for the first time in your life, that another man is actively interested in your feet.

You sit down, and your shoes are taken off. They suddenly look forlorn and rather shabby. Don't worry about it. The purveyor is not concerned with them any more; it's your feet that fascinate him. Having confirmed that there are two, of more or less the same size, he summons his acolyte, who may be a fresh-faced apprentice from the cobbler's bench or a wizened retainer. In either case he carries a large, leather-bound book, opened at two blank pages.

The open book is placed upon the floor. You are asked to stand on it, one foot per page, and the purveyor kneels before you. Slowly, almost lovingly, he makes a map of each foot by tracing the two outlines on to the pages of the book. From those nearly prehensile big toes, round the mysterious knurls that embellish the little toes, along the sides, and deep under the arches, not a single wrinkle or irregularity is left unrecorded.

Once the maps are completed, the topographical survey can begin. Everything is measured: altitude of instep, curve of heel, contours and slopes of the metatarsal range. You might even be asked if you normally wear your toe-nails that length, because millimetres count. At last you are allowed to step off the book and prepare yourself for decisions. Now is the time to choose the style of your shoe.

While the choices are almost endless, it has to be said that you will not find Cuban heels, brass snaffles, three-tone snakeskin-overlaid broguing, or anything that might be considered a trifle gaudy. You, of course, have nothing like that in mind. What you want is a classic, timeless, brown lace-up shoe. Simple.

All you have to do is decide on the leather (calf, cordovan,

crocodile, brushed deerskin); the precise shape of the toe (almond, slightly squared, standard rounded); the height of the heel (nothing too extreme, mind you, but an extra eighth of an inch might be arranged); the shaping around the arch of the foot (a chamfered waist is recommended here for a particularly smart finish); the extent of decoration (again, there are limits, but some restrained work around the toe and instep is highly acceptable); and finally, the laces (woven or leather, flat-cut or rolled). These absorbing details must not be rushed, because you will be living with the results for a long time.

You eventually take your leave of the purveyor with expressions of mutual satisfaction for a job well and thoroughly done. He looks forward to seeing you again.

But when? Several months go by without a word. And then, just as you're beginning to wonder if your order has been confused with the Duke of Glencoe's stalking boots, you receive a postcard. More baroque language, requesting the favour of a visit for a fitting, assuring you of their best attention at all times while remaining yours faithfully, and generally giving you the impression that they have come up with the goods.

Your second visit to the premises is accompanied by a pleasant familiarity. The half dozen men – the same ones you saw months ago, for all you know – are still bent in devotion over their toecaps. The difference is that you will shortly be one of them, and here to prove it is the purveyor with your shoes.

He holds them up for inspection. Two burnished offerings, the color of ox blood, with brass-hinged shoe trees – works of art themselves – growing out of them. The purveyor trusts they will be satisfactory. Good God, they're superb! And the minute you put them on, your feet assume a totally different character. They used to be frogs and have turned into princes. They have lost weight. Not only are these shoes lighter than a ready-made shoe, they are also narrower and more elegantly shaped. No wonder all those old boulevardiers spend hours staring downwards, marvelling at their aristocratic feet. You find yourself doing exactly the same.

You are tactfully interrupted by the purveyor with some practical advice. Always insert the shoe trees immediately after removing the feet, while the leather is still warm. Make sure that whoever polishes your shoes (the assumption is that it will be a minion, and not yourself) works the polish well into the join between sole and upper. And bring the shoes in every year or so for servicing. (When you do, they will be received in the same way that a nursing home welcomes a rich hypochondriac, with solicitous inquiries as to his current state of health, followed by prolonged rest and treatment.) Given this kind of undemanding maintenance, your shoes will last twenty years or more.

At current prices, therefore, you will be paying about £35 a year for the comfort of wearing shoes that really fit, and the pleasure of wearing shoes that will actually grow more handsome with age. The rituals, the ornately phrased postcards, the poring over leathers and laces and waxes and creams, and the agreeable thought that your lasts, the exact replicas of your feet, are in safe lodgings somewhere in the depths of Jermyn Street or St James's – all these are thrown in. As addictions go, this one is a bargain.

THE
BLACK
STRETCH

It all started when the world's first truly status-conscious man realized that the lowliest of his servants had exactly the same number of legs as he did. This posed a social problem – not in the privacy of the home, where the master's status was part of the furniture, but out on the road. How could the proper manifestations of importance be maintained in the confusion of a pedestrian traffic jam? Suppose someone mistook our status-conscious man for just another two-legged servant? Something had to be done.

Something was. Ingenuity came to the rescue, as it invariably does in matters of self-esteem. The status-conscious man decided that the way to show the world who was boss was to be transported in as lavish a fashion as possible. It was a notion that caught on.

Indian princelings developed the chauffeur-driven elephant, with a penthouse balanced precariously on top. In eighteenth-century Europe, competition among the crowned heads to see who could come up with the most impressive set of wheels reached fever pitch. Matched sets of pearl-grey horses, coaches with rococo panelling, flunkies, whip-wavers, outriders – it was enough to make the Detroit designs of the fifties look like models of restraint.

Fundamentally, nothing has changed. The idea of a form of transport that is at the same time highly visible to the mob and yet insulated from it remains as seductive as ever. And the most satisfying contemporary example of that is the coal-black stretch limousine. (White is vulgar, grey is a compromise banker's colour, puce and magenta and antique crackle-finish gold are not for gentleman. It has to be black.)

There is something almost indecent about using several yards of machinery and the full-time services of another human being simply to move you the short distance between lunch and your next appointment. This, of course, is one of the most emotionally rewarding aspects of travel by stretch, but not one you would necessarily want to mention to liberal acquaintances who are concerned about equality, ecology and our moral obligation to use mass transit. Better to keep that small pleasure to yourself, and to justify your limo bills on practical grounds.

These you will find in abundance. All serious limousines are fitted with the following essential items: a telephone, a bar and an electrically operated glass partition that seals off the driver where he belongs, in the engine room. (There is often a TV set as well, but who needs television when there are so many other ways to amuse yourself?)

The phone is obviously invaluable for keeping in touch with lady friends and bookmakers, but it has an important business advantage as well. Car phones, fortunately, are still not entirely free from interference. So if the conversation gets sticky or you need time to think, tell your caller that you're passing under a network of high-tension cables, whistle piercingly into the mouth-piece and hang up. Alternatively, tell him that a call has come through on the other line.

The bar. Standard supplies usually include gin, scotch and vodka. The more thoughtful limousine will also provide an ice bucket large enough for a bottle of champagne. There is comfort-able seating for five or six people. You can see at once the oppor-tunities for small mobile cocktail parties, with the driver stopping at liquor stores as the need arises. If your guests are the carefree kind who spill drinks, spray morsels of caviare on to the rug or shower the stereo system with cigar ash, at least it's done on neutral ground and not in your apartment. And you will have had fun. A good stiff drink as you cruise down Park Avenue – or North Michigan Avenue or Beacon Street – tastes even better when the view from your window is of maddened executives locking horns over who saw the cab first.

The impression of being in a pleasant cocoon, far from real life, is heightened by the decisive use of the glass partition between you and the driver. If your previous experience of partitions has been the greasy Perspex in taxis, which forces you to bellow your instructions at the driver and makes payment of the fare a process of crushed fingers and muttered oaths, the limo partition will come as a revelation to you. One touch of the button in your arm-rest and the conversation-proof glass hisses up and stops com-munication dead. (All professional drivers, for some reason, love

to chat. Don't tolerate it. You're not paying all that money to listen to a lecture on Bush's fiscal policies.)

So there you are, a million miles from those yahoos on the street, immune from the weather, protected from small talk from the cockpit, going wherever you want to go in your own controlled environment. A perfect setting for a romantic assignation.

Women love limos. The minute they settle back in the seat they feel pampered and relaxed. They mentally dab a little scent behind each knee. They take a little more to drink than usual. They tend to lean towards you and whisper. They bloom. A date in a stretch is more intimate, more impressive and far less prone to distraction than a movie and a candle-lit dinner. It is an extremely focused occasion.

A word of warning here. Whether on pleasure or business, it is important to observe chauffeur protocol, and this means curbing your natural warmth. We're not suggesting rudeness; distant politeness will do very well. In other words, don't try to shake hands with your chauffeur or ask him how he's doing. Don't encourage him to address you by your first name. And don't ever open the door yourself, even if you have to wait a minute or two while he walks down the length of the car to let you out. These boys are pros, and they respect a pro passenger.

After one or two outings, you will probably start to become more specific in your requirements. You won't want any old limo. You'll want a limo in which the details are *exactly right*. A compact-disc player instead of a tape deck. Leather upholstery rather than cloth. Single-malt scotch, a freshly ironed copy of the *Wall Street Journal*, a Fax machine, a silver vase of freesias – once you get into the refinements you'll never want to get out. But these come later.

While, as we have stated, only a black limo will do, we draw the line at black-tinted windows, for two reasons. First, they encourage autograph hunters, who will sidle up when the car is stopped at a light and peer at you and possibly mistake you for Mick Jagger or, worse, Ivan F. Boesky. And second, they make it virtually impossible for your friends – or, better still, your enemies – to catch a glimpse of you as you place phone calls and get to grips with the crystal decanters. Clear-glass windows are our recommendation, but it's a matter of personal choice.

In the stretch business, as in most other businesses, there exists a reduced price trial offer. It works like this: let's say that you find yourself in Manhattan at the corner of 55th and Third one evening around 6.30. All the cabs are taken, but if you make yourself sufficiently obvious as a man in need of transport, it won't be long before a prowling limo slows down. Hail it. Providing the driver likes the look of you, he'll stop, because he's just dropped his passenger and has a couple of hours to kill before picking him up again. Imbued with the spirit of enterprise, the driver will want to use this time profitably. As long as your destination won't make him late for his pick-up, nobody will be the wiser and he'll be a little richer. The exact price should be agreed on before you get in, but you can be sure that it will be less than a formal arrangement with the limo company.

One trip is all it will take to make you start juggling your disposable income to pay for further expeditions, until the day comes when you will be ready to enjoy the ultimate refinement: taking your stretch for a walk.

A stroll of two or three blocks on a fine spring evening, the great black beast crawling obediently to heel, the bar stocked and waiting, the chauffeur alert to your beckoning finger, a ripple of envy through less fortunate pedestrians marking your progress – now, there's a way to work up an appetite for dinner.

THE
MOST
COSTLY
PASSION
OF ALL

Unless you happen to live in one of those delightfully backward Latin countries where husbands are encouraged to form liaisons with other women instead of loitering round the house and watching TV, the mistress is forbidden fruit. She is a threat to the fabric of polite society, a wrecker of homes and a walking distraction to men who should be keeping their eye on the corporate ball. She wears black underwear. She takes long, scented baths. She sneers at housework. She is either feared or envied, or both, by fifty per cent of the married population of America. She is illicit.

It is this, more than anything else, that keeps the mistress in business, despite high running costs and savage increases in the size of the Ultimate Fine if dalliance is followed by divorce. (A process that our lawyer friend describes as working out who gets custody of the money.) If mistresses were socially acceptable, they would lose much of their appeal; it is the whiff of sin and the fear of discovery that sharpen the pleasure, make parting such sweet sorrow and enable a man to contemplate his American Express bills with a secret smile.

We shall return to those bills later, but for those of you who are about to invest in a mistress, it should be said that the costs are not just financial. Who can put a price on the emotional wear and tear caused by whispering the wrong name into the wrong ear at the wrong time? The desperate attempts to remove the lingering traces of Chanel No 5 from a suit that is supposed to have spent the evening at a sales conference? The thrill of horror as someone vaguely known and dimly seen waves at the two of you in a restaurant that *nobody* goes to? The sprint for the mailbox to collect incriminating evidence before it falls into the wrong hands? The verbal acrobatics required to cover up those deadly slips of the tongue? The marvels of contorted invention that have to be produced to explain why you didn't call to say you weren't getting back from the office until 3 a.m.?

In fact, these daily jolts of intrigue and adrenalin are meat and drink to the mistress addict. A woman is just a woman, but a mistress is an exercise in tightrope walking and ingenuity as much as a source of physical excitement. The mind loves the whole naughty business as much as the body. Which is just as well, because in simple cash terms a mistress will cost only marginally less than a forty-five-foot yacht or a promising racehorse.

There are five major areas of expenditure that prospective cads should expect. The amounts allocated to each will vary according to whim of mistress, degree of guilt, logistical complications and credit limit, so it is difficult to be precise about the bottom-line figure. However, you can be sure that it will be much more than the number you first thought of, divided more or less as follows:

Tokens of Affection

'How do I love thee?' Elizabeth Barrett Browning wrote. 'Let me count the ways.' But that was in the good old pre-inflationary days when you could not only count the ways, but afford to pay for them as well. Not any more. Modern society offers limitless opportunities to blow your salary, and your mistress will be happy to guide you through them. They range from a modest bouquet of roses that have been reared on a mulch of bank notes to ludicrously expensive scraps of silk masquerading as underwear, and onwards and upwards to Cartier, Van Cleef and Arpels and floor-length sable coats, until you arrive, if your passion and resources can run to it, at the most acceptable trinket of all: the love nest. Nothing brings the bloom to a mistress's cheek like real estate, preferably in a high-rent district and (for discretion's sake, of course) with her name on the lease.

Remodelling Expenses

Men with newly acquired mistresses frequently undergo a transformation almost as startling as the frog-into-handsome-prince routine. They go on diets. They buy dashing ties and bottom-hugging Italian suits. They have their hair styled. They seriously consider trading in the station wagon for something low and aerodynamic and dangerous-looking. They change their no-nonsense aftershave for a musk-based lounge-lizard concoction

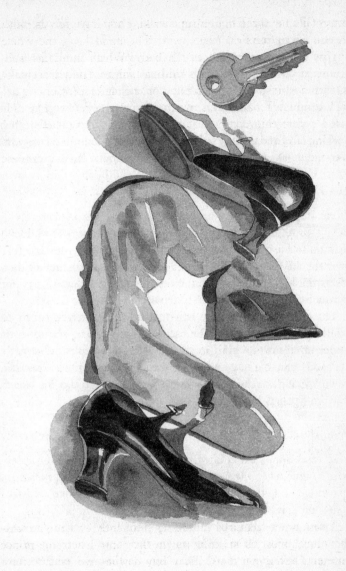

that retails for three figures an ounce. They leave for the office dressed for romance.

This does not pass unnoticed. Our man may think his explanations are plausible, but he's kidding himself. His secretary will know almost instantly what's going on, but at least (assuming he's not a complete scoundrel) he won't be sharing a bed with her. His wife is a different matter. She trusts him. She *wants* to believe he's working late, and as his excuses become more and more flimsy, he becomes more and more guilty, leading directly to the next expense.

Remorse Gifts

Wives of men with mistresses often find themselves on the receiving end of unsolicited and puzzling gifts. Benign neglect suddenly changes to husbandly concern. Health, leisure activities and relatives are the favourite topics, but it doesn't matter which of these scams the husband chooses; the end result is the same – an offer of an all-expense-paid trip to somewhere far away.

Thus it happens that the bewildered wife is packed off to the health spa at Eugenie-Les-Bains, to a hang-gliding course in the Andes or to visit an aunt in upstate Alaska. Needless to say, the husband is unable to go with her due to his obligations – pressure of work being one, and a long-standing promise to take his sweetie to Palm Springs being the other.

Provisions

Mistresses do not eat at Burger Barn. They do not drink beer. And after a while, even the most extravagant picnics in hotel rooms and apartments lose their novelty. There comes a time when a mistress insists on going out to eat, and this creates its own problems.

A restaurant has to be safe to be suitable. How can you enjoy the touch of a silken knee under the table when you're half expecting to bump into your next-door neighbours? You are therefore limited to restaurants that the people you know never visit, and for a very good reason: they can't afford to.

As you look down the menu and blink in disbelief at asparagus that is priced by the inch and at £30 lamb chops, you recall a charming compliment paid to you by your companion: she *loves* your carefree attitude with money. Fiscal restraint is out of the question, and to make sure you don't escape for less than £150, here comes that smirking bastard with the wine list.

Experienced wine waiters can recognise a clandestine couple from a distance of twelve feet. The subtler operators will hand you the wine list open at the champagne page. The hustlers will suggest it – not to you, but to her – confident in the knowledge that mistresses can't resist champagne.

Add to that the Grand Marnier soufflé, the 1929 cognac and the double-digit tip (generous to the last, and you might want to come back) and you have a bill suitable for framing.

Transportation

Mistresses don't have cars because they don't need them. Public transportation is something they once read about in the paper. Your car is too risky and occupies attentions that are better directed elsewhere. Taxis are dirty, driven by garrulous maniacs and generally unromantic. You have no real choice but the limousine.

It all mounts up.

THE
GENUINE
£1000
FOLDING
HAT

The man in the hat is something of a rarity these days, and I think it's a pity. Hats are stylish and elegant, and they speak volumes about the personality of the wearer. Should you think of yourself as a budding financier, a boulevardier, a closet gangster, a cowboy by nature if not by profession – all this and more can be hinted at by what you put on your head. Indeed, hats have often become individual trade marks, as much a part of a man's appearance as his nose. Think of Winston Churchill, Humphrey Bogart, the Marlboro man, early Frank Sinatra or Crocodile Dundee, and the chances are that they will step into your imagination wearing their hats.

Quite apart from its aesthetic qualities, a hat is practical. It will keep your head warm in the winter, cool in the summer, unruffled in the wind, dry in the rain. But what do we see on the head of the modern man? Either nothing, or an adjustable, impersonal, plastic and nylon baseball cap advertising beer.

I'm as guilty and bareheaded as the next man, but I do love hats as decorative objects, and I have a rack of them at home on the wall: an Australian bush hat, a couple of fedoras, a fez for festive occasions and, for the use of summer guests, half a dozen Panamas in varying stages of decrepitude. Still graceful despite years of rough treatment, they have turned a faded, buttery colour, and to look at them in winter brings back pleasant memories of hot days and cool drinks.

I had never stopped to think too much about the differences between one Panama and another. Some have wider brims or higher crowns, a crease in the middle or dents in the front, but otherwise they are just good-looking, lightweight hats of approximately the same quality. Or so I thought.

I could have carried my ignorance to the grave if a friend – knowing of my interest in anything preposterously extravagant – hadn't told me about a hat that cost £1000. But not a solid, indestructible, waterproof lifetime investment of a hat. This was a mere straw. Who would be lunatic enough to pay out four figures for less than three ounces which you would hardly know you had on your head?

By coincidence, I had to go to London shortly after hearing about this featherweight phenomenon, and I was curious to see it. So I made an appointment with Anthony Marangos, who runs the venerable firm of Herbert Johnson, hatters to the gentry since 1790.

As Mr Marangos escorted me on a tour through the silk toppers and buckshot-proof tweed shooting caps, the ink-black bowlers and tasselled velvet smoking hats, he made discreet mention of some of the better-known Herbert Johnson customers. The royal head of Prince Charles was at the top of the list, followed by the officers and gentlemen of most of the smartest regiments in the British Army. This was impressive, but no great surprise, coming as it did from a hatter of 200 years' standing. What I didn't know was that the little workroom at the back of the shop also produces custom-designed hats for some of the most eminent figures from Hollywood and Broadway. Indiana Jones, Inspector Clouseau, Professor Henry Higgins and The Joker – all of these and many others have been given their final sartorial touch by Herbert Johnson.

By now, we were approaching the corner of the shop where the sun never sets, or never on an uncovered head, at any rate. Here were the Bombay bowlers and tropical pith helmets and the hat that I had come to see: the ultimate, genuine, foldable king's ransom Panama.

The first step in my education was that Panama hats don't come from Panama. They are hand woven from toquilla straw (at night, so the story goes, when it's cooler) in the foothills of Ecuador. The misleading name came about because the hats were worn by workers on the Panama Canal. They would proably have made do with a basic, relatively coarsely woven model, but in fact there are altogether twenty grades of Panama.

'Hold this one up to the light,' said Mr Marangos. 'See the rings? The closer they are, the tighter the weave.' And the higher the price, naturally, although the hat I was looking at was only a modest £150 or so. It felt very good – wafer-thin,

crisp and comfortable – and I wondered how much better the millionaire's version could be.

My education continued. The best of all Panama hats come from the town of Montecristi, and the pride of Montecristi is the *fino*. A single hat can take as long as three months to make, and with properly respectful use will last for twenty years. These statistics, however, didn't prepare me in any way for the experience of handling a Montecristi *fino* for the first time.

It was floated on to the table in front of me – a pale, well-bred cream, with a dark grey band and a pronounced ridge running from the front of the crown to the back. It felt extraordinary, more like thick silk than straw, and the weave was so fine and dense that it was hard to believe the hat had started life as a fistful of separate strands.

It had arrived in London, like all of Herbert Johnson's Panamas, as a plain cone, unformed and untrimmed. In the workshop, it had been given its shape, its central ridge, its Cheltenham band (which might, in less discriminating establishments, be called the sweatband) and its outer band. This, I was told, could be changed to suit the owner's whim, from club colours to polka dots. Or a favourite tie, re-cut and promoted to hatband status.

I held the hat up to the light and looked inside. More rings than I could easily count, and at the top of the crown, two sets of faint initials to identify the craftsmen who had been responsible for the masterpiece. What a piece of work. I was feeling the first stirrings of temptation as Mr Marangos let me in on a ghastly trade secret. Not every hat that looks like a Panama and is sold as a Panama is the real thing. Artful fakes are everywhere, often coming from the Orient, and sometimes made from nothing more substantial than straw-coloured paper. Try folding one of those up, he said with a sniff, and that would be the end of your hat.

Ah yes, the folding. I had almost forgotten that one of the charming characteristics of the true top-quality Panama is its astonishing suppleness, which allows you to fold it in half and roll it into a cone slim enough to pass through a wedding ring.

While you may not want to perform this party trick very often, it does mean that you can slip your Panama into a tube for travelling and unpack it later without the trace of a wrinkle.

I asked for a demonstration, and watched as the hat – I was definitely beginning to think of it as *my* hat – became a cone in about five seconds. A slow-motion replay allowed me to see exactly how it was done. The hat is placed against the stomach, and folded in half down its central ridge. Two or three turns of the wrist, and you have your cone. A gentle shake, and you get your hat back, miraculously uncreased. Simple.

'You might need one of these as well,' said Mr Marangos. He produced a handsome maroon tube with the Herbert Johnson coat of arms picked out in gold. 'For your travels.' The rolled-up hat was an exact fit.

I thought about it. Did I need a hat like this, after so many years of going without? Probably not. Could I afford a hat like this, costing more than its weight in dollar bills? Certainly not. What would my accountant say when I tried to justify it as an office expense? It didn't bear thinking about.

'Fine,' I heard myself say. 'I'll take it.'

I'LL BE SUING YOU

I t is normally my pleasant duty to report on the little extrava-
gances that make life worth living and a dollar worth earning –
the civilised rewards available to anyone with a healthy streak
of self-indulgence and a good credit rating. This month, however,
we shall be looking at one expensive habit – alas, becoming more
widespread every day – that offers no enjoyment of any kind to
the millions of poor wretches who are forced to pay for it. In
theory, it is the pursuit of justice. In practice, it consists of handing
over large sums of money to the kind of people you wouldn't want
to meet in your neighbourhood bar.

There is something horribly wrong with a world in which there
are more lawyers than good chefs, and yet every year the law
schools unleash a further plague of them, letting them loose on
the streets to jabber about malpractice, malfeasance, alimony,
palimony, torts and suits and God knows what else, causing dread
and apprehension in the hearts of simple, honest citizens like you
and me. Indeed, there are several office buildings in mid-town
Manhattan (lawyers have a liking for choice real estate) where you
risk an injunction merely by stepping on someone's foot in a
crowded elevator. The foot turns out to be attached to a pillar of
the legal profession, and before you know it you're facing charges
of attempted grievous bodily harm as defined in and pursuant to
the case of *Schulz v. Donoghue*, 1923.

I am not alone in my misgivings. Lawyers have been the object
of heartfelt invective ever since man developed the intelligence to
spell 'litigation'. 'A peasant between two lawyers is like a fish
between two cats,' says the Spanish proverb. 'Lawyers and painters
can soon change black to white,' says the Danish proverb. 'The
first thing we do, let's kill all the lawyers,' says Shakespeare.
Benjamin Franklin, Thoreau, Emerson and many other good men
and true have also expressed themselves in pungent and unflattering terms on the subject of our learned friends. How can it be,
then, that despite centuries of well deserved unpopularity there
are more of them around than ever before?

There are many contributory factors, but perhaps the most basic is the language problem. For their own obvious ends, lawyers have perfected an exclusive form of communication. It has a passing resemblance to English mixed with a smattering of dog Latin, but to the man in the street, it might just as well be Greek. Thus, when he receives a writ or a subpoena or one of the other countless arrows in the legal quiver, he is completely mystified. What does it mean? What can he do? What else but hire an interpreter – who is, of course, a lawyer. And there we have the kind of situation that lawyers love: the two sides can settle down to a protracted exchange of mumbo-jumbo, most of it unintelligible to their clients and all of it charged at an hourly rate that defies belief.

Then there is the law, not made by man but dictated by human nature, that requires that idle hands find mischievous employment. When there is not enough work for the legal population, you might reasonably expect the number of lawyers to decrease, with the less successful leaving to try their luck at something useful, like plumbing. Not a chance. If there is not enough work to go around, more work is created. Subdivisions of the law and their specialists spring up to make daily life more complicated for us and more remunerative for them. The result is that you find yourself having to deal with not one lawyer but a whole platoon of them.

The first, let's say, specialises in real estate. He will uncover the booby traps hidden (by another lawyer) in the fine print of your apartment lease. You will need a second to explain the subtleties built into your contract of employment, a third if you should disagree with the Inland Revenue about the size of your contributions to the national economy, a fourth if your doctor makes a slip of the scalpel, a fifth if you get divorced, a sixth ... But the list is already too long and too depressing, and we haven't even begun to venture into criminal law or that most overpopulated branch of an overpopulated profession, corporate law. Lawyers are everywhere except under the bed, and that might not be too far away if their numbers continue to increase.

And why do we need them? Self-defence. Because the other side – be it landlord, employer, ex-wife or whoever – has elected to have a long and expensive argument rather than a quick, cheap one, and has retained a professional representative to do it. It's no good thinking that you, a rank amateur, can conduct you own case. Innocence will get you nowhere these days, and ignorance will cost you dear. You wouldn't be able to understand more than one word in ten anyway. There is no alternative but to fight fire with fire and to employ your own legal bodyguard.

So we have to assume that lawyers are necessary. But that doesn't explain why they are so heartily detested, so frequently reviled and even, dare I say it, distrusted. To understand why these attitudes exist, we must look into the mind of the beast himself and see what it is that makes the lawyer tick.

His guiding principle, drummed into him from his first days as a callow student, is never, under any circumstances, to admit to being wrong, partly because his professional reputation for omniscience would suffer and partly because it might expose him to the awful possibility of a negligence suit. Now, it is obviously easier to avoid being wrong if you can avoid stating a clear opinion that may later prove to be arrant nonsense. This is why there is great fondness in legal circles for two well-tried secret weapons that have enabled generations of lawyers to retain the appearance of wisdom without the effort of original thought.

The vaguer of the two is the Grey Area, into which the lawyer dives like a rabbit down a burrow if anyone should threaten him with a loaded question. On the face of it, he says, you seem to have a strong case. He nods encouragingly and peers at you over the top of his half-glasses. But there are some aspects of it, some mitigating factors, some imponderables, one or two possible extenuations – no, it's not quite as cut and dried as it looks to the layman. In fact, he says, this particular instance is rather a Grey Area.

The law, as you subsequently discover if you're unfortunate enough to be involved with it often, is almost entirely made up of Grey Areas, and they are deeply, deeply valued for providing opportunities to say absolutely nothing in a highly professional manner. The only glimmers of clarity in this fog of obfuscation occur when your case happens to be an exact replica of another case on which judgment was pronounced fifty years ago and hasn't been challenged since. This is when the second secret weapon is triumphantly produced.

Precedent! What a wonderful labour-saving, *definitive* thing it is. When a lawyer is stuck for an answer, he consults precedent. When he wants to flatten an opponent, he quotes precedent. When he disagrees with some proposed legal novelty, he argues that there's no precedent for it. But what exactly is precedent? Somebody's opinion, grown old and respectable with the passage of time, but still only an opinion. 'Precedent' is probably the most popular word in the legal dictionary, and it has a great advantage over the Grey Area because it permits lawyers to be decisive without having to take any responsibility for the decision.

But enough of these disparaging comments on the devious nature of the legal personality. Let us now move on to the matter of fees and costs, because it is here more than anywhere that the ordinary man's attitude towards the legal man changes from mild suspicion to violent outrage.

We have all read about cases where the costs run into hundreds of thousands of dollars and the settlements into millions. But those figures are so ridiculously overblown, like the budget deficit, that is impossible to take them seriously. They're not real. They do, however, provide us with dramatic examples of that compulsion, common to all lawyers, for extracting every last cent from a situation. This is not necessarily to make the punishment fit the crime or to put a true and proper value on justice. It is the natural and inevitable consequence of the pound of flesh mentality.

All lawyers have it. They can't help it; it's in their genes, and it shows itself at every level from the multi-million dollar lawsuit down to the smallest, most fleeting incident. If a pound of flesh isn't immediately available, a couple of ounces will suffice. I myself have been charged £150 for a cup of coffee and a ten-minute chat, but at least the chat took place in an office. A friend of mine was actually billed for a phone call he made to his lawyer inviting him out to dinner. I didn't ask if there was a further charge for time spent eating the free dinner, but it wouldn't have surprised me.

I don't have the exact figures, but I am told that the current growth rate in the legal profession is, in relative terms, far greater than the growth in population. Lawyers are being hatched like chickens, and it is only a matter of time before the entire country is overrun. Everywhere will become like those parts of Los Angeles where lawyers outnumber people. The more affluent families will have live-in attorneys. Litigation, once the hobby of the rich, will take over from baseball and football as a leisure activity, and Berlitz will offer courses in Legalese. I have seen the future, and it's a Grey Area.

6

WHICH SIDE DO YOU DRESS?

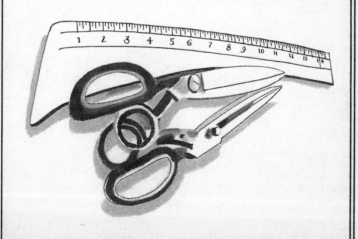

Of the many small indignities that we have to suffer in life, perhaps one of the most expensive and deflating is our first visit to a bespoke tailor – particularly one of those London tailors whose forebears made breeches for Lord Nelson or moiré hunting underwear for the Prince Regent. There they stand, these lords of the cloth, corseted in sixteen-ounce worsted, surrounded by mahogany wainscoting and framed bills (probably still unpaid) for Oscar Wilde's frock coats, waiting for innocents like you and me who feel the urge for a hand-made suit.

They run a polite but disparaging eye over you and what you have always thought to be your smartest outfit, worn specially for the occasion. 'Yes,' they murmur eventually, 'I think we can do a little better than *that*.'

Having destroyed your suit, they settle down to the serious business of recording your physical curiosities. This is a practised double act: the man with the tape measure and the cryptic comments, and his scribe, who notes your defects in a large book, already bulging with past deformities. It isn't overtly insulting. It's simply as if you were a deaf, inanimate and inconveniently shaped object to be shrouded as tastefully as possible.

Many of the comments are unfamiliar. None of them sounds flattering. Trying desperately to remain impassive, you eavesdrop and hear about things you never knew you had: a dropped left shoulder, a slipped chest, slight lordosis in the lower back, the suspicion of a hump, legs of unequal length – 'Do we *normally* stand like that, sir?' – and several other revelations too ghastly to commit to print.

By this time, your main concern is to get to a doctor as quickly as possible, but duty calls. You must now choose your cloth and make vital decisions about buttons, flaps, vents, lapels, stitching – all those delightfully arcane details that make a hand-made suit so much more satisfying than clothes tailored in a factory. It should be a deeply enjoyable experience, lasting for an hour or two and leaving you in the mood for a glass of champagne. But unfortunately, the shock of discovering that you are nothing but a human potato with posture problems has left you demoralised, with your decisive powers in paralysis. Feeble and unprotesting, you are steered firmly by the tailor into the standard establishment suit. Better made, certainly, than your previous suits, but somehow not quite what you had in mind.

After my first hand-made suit, I retired, hurt, for several years. And yet, every once in a while, the urge would return to spend a morning among the swatches and discuss horn buttons with someone sympathetic who wouldn't make me feel like a basket case with a cheque book.

Did such a tailor exist? Yes, he did, according to George, the elegant London antique dealer. George and his tailor had a rapport that went far beyond the perfunctory measuring of an inside leg and the exchange of clothes for money. George and his tailor were friends, and George's suits were the best-looking I had ever seen. I wanted one. No, I wanted half a dozen. Most of all, I wanted a tailor I could feel at ease with. And so I took my dropped left shoulder, my lordosis and my legs of unequal length along to 95 Mount Street in Mayfair to meet Douglas Hayward.

His shop is in complete contrast to the wainscoting and dusty-relic school of decor still favoured by the elders of the tailoring business. It's more like a living room, except that the shelves are filled with shirts and ties and sweaters instead of books. There are invariably one or two people sitting round exchanging jokes and insults. Music comes from the cutting room in the back. Anguished phone calls come from clients who have had one lunch too many and need their trousers let out. Black London cabs come to ferry suits to Claridges or the Dorchester or the Los Angeles flight from Heathrow. Sales representatives come for a five-minute call with their wool and linen and cashmere and leather, and stay for half an hour and a cup of tea. It is not in the least daunting, and I say that as one who's daunted very easily.

Hayward himself is as relaxed as his shop. Unlike most tailors, who wear suits of such rigid perfection that they don't look real, he is handsomely dressed in clothes that can clearly cope with the normal range of bodily movements. (Some English tailors, to this day, are so conscious of their heritage of eighteenth-century

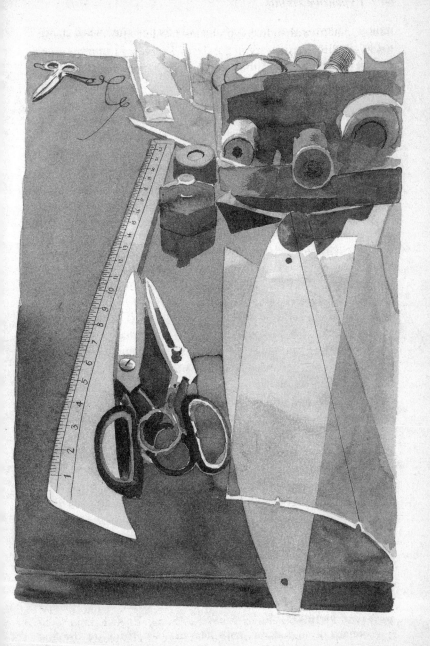

military tailoring that their suits are only really happy when standing at attention.)

The next pleasant surprise is that you are never aware of being inspected for sartorial crimes. You can turn up for a fitting in shorts and a Hawaiian shirt without raising any eyebrows. I once saw a customer dressed only in shirt, tie and jacket, having a cup of coffee while his trousers were being pressed in the back room. In this sort of atmosphere, it is almost impossible not to feel at home. The process of ordering a suit is therefore what it should be – that is, informal, friendly and unhurried. It happens more or less like this.

Your first visit will probably last about an hour. Most of this time will be spent chatting with Hayward. By the time the tape measure finally comes out, he will have some ideas about cloth and cut. Unless you have very precise requirements – and most men don't – it is always best to go along with what he suggests. Someone has to be in charge of the suit, and he's better at it than you are.

He takes you into the back to be measured. The process is as devoid of trauma as anything involving waist measurement can be, because by now you're discussing the respective merits of hopsack or flannel, raised seams, side vents, concealed ticket pockets and that most intimate of matters – whether your genitals prefer to be housed to the east or the west of the zip. In tailoring language, this is called dressing to the left or the right, and an extra accommodation is made in the appropriate trouser leg. As you can imagine, with all this going on, you are far too busy to notice the muttered instructions that are being jotted down in the book. The ordeal by tape measure is painless.

With the measurements taken, the cloth chosen and the style agreed upon, you leave Hayward to get on with it. He cuts your pattern and the actual material. His assistants assemble and stitch. Suits are made on the premises. (In fact, having served his time as a tailor's apprentice, Hayward can make the entire suit by himself, which is rare and becoming rarer. There are now only four tailors' apprentices in the West End of London, where there were once hundreds).

A month or so goes by, and then you come back for the first

fitting. This can be surprising unless you know what to expect, because no sooner are you casting a discreetly admiring eye at your reflection in the mirror than Hayward pounces on you, mouth bristling with pins, and rips the sleeves from the jacket. There follows a few hectic minutes of adjusting and pinning and scrawling hieroglyphics here and there on the suit with tailor's chalk before he stands back in the manner of a sculptor casting a critical eye over a promising but unfinished chunk of marble. One final twitch of the chalk, and you and your suit part company until the next fitting. The suit will now be taken apart completely, seams pressed flat, adjustments made according to the coded chalk marks and then put together again, this time with the finished hand stitching that is one of the subtle but unmistakable marks of bespoke tailoring. A second fitting takes care of any vestigial tucks and wrinkles. (The entire process requires about six weeks, less for subsequent orders. Informal deliveries are made to the United States whenever Hayward goes to New York or Los Angeles. He usually arrives with twenty suits over his arm for American clients.)

Then the suit's all yours. You don't even have to look in the mirror. It feels right. It feels comfortable. What it doesn't feel is new. There is minimal padding in the shoulders, and none of that stiff and cumbersome upholstery around the chest that makes so many London stockbrokers look like stuffed pinstriped fish. That's not to say your suit will be, in the currently fashionable way, 'unconstructed'. It will have a graceful, almost fleshy roll to the lapel. It will sit smoothly on your shoulders. It will fit snugly at the back of the neck, where poorly cut suits always have a ridge. The buttons on the sleeves will undo, as buttons should. There will be a tiny loop behind the left lapel to anchor the stem of the carnation in your buttonhole. In other words, it will be a very *constructed* suit. But comfortable.

It will also make you look slightly thinner and an inch or two taller than you look in less well fitting suits. And as long as you don't want to look like a rumpled parachute one season and an extra from *Brideshead Revisited* the next, you will be wearing your suit with increasing pleasure over the next fifteen or twenty years. It won't date. Hayward doesn't make extreme clothes.

Alas, he doesn't make inexpensive clothes, either. Suit prices start at about £800, jackets at £500. Which brings us to the one area where Hayward and traditional tailors have something in common. When I asked him what was the single most difficult part of making suits for gentlemen, he didn't hesitate for a second. 'Getting paid,' he said. It is ever thus between men and tailors.

THE MILLIONAIRE'S MUSHROOM

E arly, on a raw winter morning in Provence. The café in the small village is doing a brisk trade in breakfast jolts of marc and calvados. Strangers coming through the door bring muttered conversations to an abrupt stop. Outside, men stand in tight, unsociable groups, stamping their feet against the cold and looking, sniffing and finally weighing something that is handled with almost reverential care. Money passes, fat, grimy wads of it, in 100-, 200-, and 500-franc notes, which are double checked with much licking of thumbs and glancing over shoulders.

It is less than a two-hour reckless drive from Marseilles, and your first thought is that you have stumbled upon a gathering of rustic smack runners. In fact, it is unlikely that these gentlemen know, or care, about dope in any form. They are dealing in a perfectly legal substance, although their marketing methods may from time to time be questionable. They are selling, at outrageous prices, wart-encrusted, earth-covered lumps of fungi. They are traders in fresh truffles.

This informal market is an early stage in a process that leads to the tables of three-star restaurants and the counters of frantically chic Parisian delicatessens such as Fauchon and Hédiard. But even here, in the middle of nowhere – buying direct from men with dirt under their fingernails and yesterday's garlic on their breath, with dented, wheezing cars, with old baskets or plastic bags instead of Vuitton attaché cases – even here, the prices are, as they say, *très sérieux*. Truffles are sold by weight, and the standard unit is the kilo. This year, a kilo of truffles bought in the village market will cost you at least 2,000 francs, or £200, and you will have to pay in cash. Cheques are not accepted, receipts are never given, because the *truffiste* is not eager to participate in the crackpot government scheme the rest of us call taxation.

So the starting price is 2,000 francs a kilo. With a little nudging along the way from various agents and middlemen, by the time the truffle reaches its spiritual home in the kitchens of Bocuse or Troisgros, the price will probably have doubled. Or, if you are a prosperous and confident cook, you can always drop in to Fauchon on your way home and pay 6,000 francs a kilo. (They accept cheques.)

There are several reasons why these seemingly unrealistic prices continue to be paid, and continue to rise each year. The first and most basic is that nothing in the world smells or tastes like fresh truffles except fresh truffles. One small specimen not even the size of a walnut is enough to transform the flavour of an entire dish. The aroma has been described as 'divine, and slightly suspect, like everything that smells really good'. It is also astonishingly pervasive. It can find its way through folds of paper, even plastic. A whiff is all you need; to inhale a more concentrated dose is too much and could put you off all thoughts of eating, so heavy and rich-rotten is the smell. But used with discretion, the truffle is an incomparable treat, and lives up to Brillat-Savarin's description: 'a luxury of *grands seigneurs* and kept women'. (The nineteenth-century gastronome was presumably referring to the truffle's reputation as an aphrodisiac, which has yet to be scientifically verified.)

Today, with all the sophisticated techniques of planned cultivation at our disposal, you would think that truffles could be grown to order, cropped like any other delicacy and sold with several zeros knocked off the price. God knows, the French are trying; you will quite often come across fields in Vaucluse that some optimist has planted with truffle oaks and 'keep off' notices. But the propagation of truffles seems to be a haphazard affair that is understood only by nature – thus adding to the rarity and the price – and human attempts at truffle breeding haven't come to much. Until they do, there is only one way to get your hands on fresh truffles without spending a fortune, and that's the old-fashioned way.

It involves timing, knowledge, patience and either a pig or a trained hound. Truffles grow a few inches under the ground, near the roots of certain oak or hazelnut trees. During the season, from November until March, they can be tracked down by nose, provided you possess sensitive enough equipment. The most effective truffle detector is the pig, which is born with a fondness for the taste, and whose sense of smell in this case is superior to the dog's. Alas, the pig is not content to wag his tail and point when

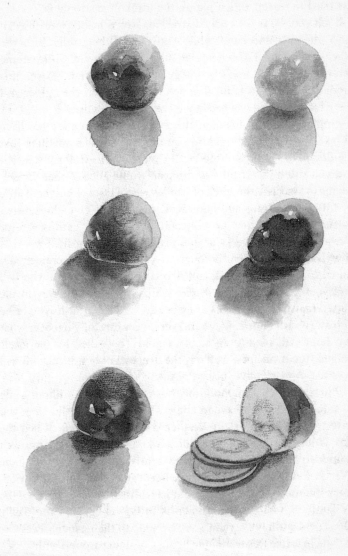

he has discovered a truffle: he wants to eat it. And, as anyone who has tried to reason with a pig on the brink of gastronomic ecstasy will tell you, he is not easily distracted. Nor is he of a size you can fend off with one hand while you rescue the truffle with the other. There are 120 pounds or more of him, rigid with porcine determination. He won't be budged, try as you might. Given this fundamental design fault, it is not surprising that the lighter and more tractable dog has become increasingly popular.

Unlike pigs, dogs do not instinctively seek out truffles; they have to be trained for the work. So you start by taking something that the dog likes – a slice of the locally cured *saucisson*, for instance – and you rub it on a truffle or dip it in truffle juice so that the dog begins to associate the smell of truffles with a taste of heaven. Little by little, or by leaps and bounds if you're lucky enough to own a particularly smart dog, he will come to share your enthusiasm for truffles until, after weeks or months, he is ready for field work. If your training has been thorough, if your dog is temperamentally suited to the task in hand, and if you know where to go, you will find yourself with a *chien truffier* which can point the way to the buried treasure. Then, just as he begins to scratch for it, you bribe him away with more sausage and very, very carefully uncover what you hope will be a lump of black gold. (So called by the locals because the inside of a truffle is the deepest, richest black you will ever see. A black olive, placed next to a truffle, looks pallid.)

There is a third method, for those unfortunates without a pig or a dog. Again, you have to know where to go, but this time you have to wait for the right weather conditions as well. When the sun is shining on the roots of a likely looking oak, approach cautiously and, with a stick, prod gently around the base of the tree. If a startled fly should rise vertically from the vegetation, mark the spot and dig. You might have disturbed a member of the fly family whose genetic passion is to lay its eggs on the truffle (doubtless adding a certain *je ne sais quoi* to the flavour). Peasants in Vaucluse like this technique because walking around with a stick is less conspicuous than walking around with a pig and secrecy can be more easily preserved. Truffle hunters, like good journalists, protect their sources.

It is, as you can see, a labour-intensive, unpredictable and rather murky business. And nowhere is the murk thicker than in the sales and distribution department. Admittedly, there hasn't been a truffle scandal to compare with that unpleasantness in Bordeaux a few years ago, but nevertheless there is talk that not every transaction is conducted with scrupulous honesty. Any prospective customer indelicate enough to mention these mischievous rumours to a truffle man is likely to be answered by an innocent shrug of disbelief that human nature could sink so low. It is, therefore, with no verifiable facts whatsoever that I report the following alleged truffle scams.

The first, should it ever have happened, would be virtually impossible to prove. With everything edible in France, certain areas have the reputation for producing the best. Nyons produces the best olives, Dijon the best mustard, Cavaillon the best melons, Normandy the best cream, and so on. The best truffles, it is generally agreed, come from the Périgord region of south-western France. Naturally, one pays more for them. But how do you know that the truffle you buy in Cahors hasn't been dug up several hundred kilometres away in Vaucluse? Unless you know and trust your supplier, you can't be sure. One estimate puts the figure of 'naturalised' truffles sold in Périgord but born elsewhere as high as fifty per cent.

Then there is the mysterious phenomenon of the truffle that somehow gains weight between leaving the ground and arriving on the scales. It could be that it has been giftwrapped in an extra coating of earth. On the other hand, it is possible that a heavier substance altogether has somehow found its way inside the truffle itself – invisible until, in mid-slice, your knife lays bare a sliver of metal.

After hearing stories like these, you may decide to leave the purchase of fresh truffles to the experts and take the safer option of buying your truffles in a can. You will sacrifice some of the flavour, but they will still taste good, and they will certainly still be expensive. What they may not be, however, is French. It has been hinted that some French cans with French labels actually contain Italian or Spanish truffles. If this is true, it must be the most profitable and least publicised act of co-operation ever between Common Market countries.

And yet, despite whispers of chicanery and prices that become more ridiculous each year, the French continue to follow their noses and dig into their pockets, occasionally with a generosity of spirit and a delight in gastronomy that is worth recording.

Here is an example.

My favourite local restaurant is, for the moment, unspoiled by the attentions of the *Guide Michelin* inspectors, perhaps because it is also the village bar and the headquarters of the *boules* club, and not sufficiently upholstered or pompous. Old men play cards in the front; clients of the restaurant eat in the back, and they eat food that in my experience is at least up to one-star standard. Prices are correct. The owner cooks; Madame, his wife, takes the orders; other members of the family help at the tables and in the kitchen. It is a comfortable neighbourhood restaurant with no apparent intention of hopping aboard the culinary merry-go-round that turns talented cooks into brand names and pleasant restaurants into temples of the expense account.

The chef is a sucker for fresh truffles. He has his suppliers, and he pays, as everyone must, in cash, without the benefit of a receipt. For him, this is a substantial and legitimate business cost that cannot be set against his profits, because there is no supporting evidence on paper to account for the outlay. Also, he refuses to raise his prices to a level that will offend his clientèle – even when the dishes are studded with truffles. (In winter, in Provence, the clientèle is local and careful. The silly money doesn't usually come down until Easter.)

I went there to eat one cold night in December. On the serving table was a copper pan containing several thousand francs' worth of truffles. On the menu was the chef's fresh truffle omelette. Madame was doing her best to be philosophical about the disparity between the cost of the raw material and the price on the menu, and I asked her why her husband did it. A shrug – shoulders and eyebrows going up, corners of the mouth turning down. '*Pour faire plaisir* (to make people happy),' she said. I had the omelette. It was better than sublime.

Note for supporters of white truffles: since the best of these come from Piedmont, since Piedmont is by a geographical mistake in Italy, and since the French are chauvinists down to the ground and beneath, the white truffle is not given the same respect here as is its black cousin.

DEAR
OLD
THINGS

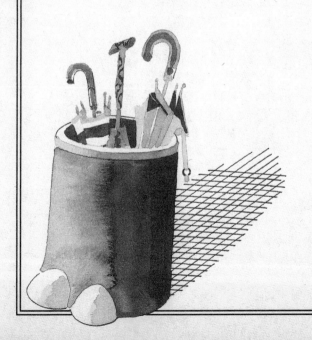

It has become a minor sport. From the artfully decorated boutiques of SoHo and Greenwich Village to the flea markets of London and Paris, from upstate New York to the rolling tarmac of Los Angeles, hundreds of thousands of hopeful and acquisitive people spend their weekend afternoons sifting through the relics of other people's houses. Indeed, so popular has the sport become that it has spawned its own ungainly verb. We go antiquing.

What is the allure of eighteenth-century chamber pots, worm-eaten armoires, gloomy Victorian portraits of fat naked nymphs, cracked and fuzzy mirrors? Do we need, in our comfortable and well equipped homes, an umbrella stand made from an elephant's hind leg? A refectory table with a one in ten gradient? A battered saucepan that is guaranteed to wobble? A spittoon? A sconce? No, of course we don't need them. But we snap them up – often at ridiculous prices – and congratulate ourselves on our good taste and keen eye. This ancient object, encrusted with grime, smelling of a hundred years' of dust and in need of a complete overhaul, is a *great buy*.

A flourishing international industry has grown up to service our magpie instincts, shipping dressers from Wales to California, quilts from Pennsylvania to Geneva, cherubs from Italy to Manhattan – criss-crossing the Atlantic, with a few zeros added to their prices each time they change hands. And still we buy. But why?

The reason most commonly given is a tribute to man's eternal optimism (which history has proved to be a dangerously misguided sentiment): we believe we're getting a bargain. Other people make expensive mistakes, but not us, even though all our experience tells us that bargains are as thin on the ground as free lunches are.

And if, in the face of a friend's disbelief at the price we paid for an Art Nouveau coat-rack, our conviction about the short-term-bargain theory should falter, we can always fall back on the long-term-investment excuse. Maybe it seems like a lot of money now, but just you wait five years. According to the dealer (a professional optimist with a fine disregard for architectural possibilities), coat-racks are ready to go through the roof.

There is always a chance that they will and that a few hundred dollars will turn into a few thousand dollars. But unless you happen to be in the business of buying and selling, that is not the real motivation. The true antique addict is an amateur in the proper sense of the word. He does it for love, as a pleasant indulgence, as a hobby that rewards him with a number of satisfactions.

The first of these is a preference for the old over the new. Naturally, the antique pine chest of drawers won't be as functional as something that was put together last week in a factory in North Carolina; it will be a little warped, the drawers will stick, the knobs will come off. Despite all that, it has a charm that can't be reproduced, which compensates for its eccentricities. The wood has the glow and smoothness that come from years of use. The shape is not quite regular, because it was cut and planed and finished by hand. It has a little of the maker's personality in it, and that makes it unique.

So you decide to buy it. And this – the foreplay leading up to the purchase – is a pleasure in itself for the amateur. Putting aside for the moment his role as connoisseur of all that is old and beautiful, he becomes the hard-nosed haggler, the prince of nego-tiators, the bargain-hunter *extraordinaire* – or he would, if he could understand the gibberish that is written on the price tag.

It is a tiresome habit of many antique dealers to mark their prices in code. Sometimes it is a straightforward substitution of letters for numerals, so that A equals 1, D equals 4, and so on. More often, the letters are given complicated values that make no sense at all to anyone other than the dealer, and so we find that our chest of drawers is clearly marked 'XPT'.

What does that mean? Would he accept XOS in cash for a quick sale? Why can't the rascal mark his prices in dollars and cents like they do at Bloomingdale's? What is he playing at?

The game is called 'matching the price to the customer'. While you have been looking at the chest of drawers, the dealer has been looking at you, and you're both considering the same question – how much? – from different points of view. Depending on how you're dressed, how interested you seem to be in buying and how interested he is in selling, the price might fluctuate significantly.

But you're not to know that. It is one of the dealer's little secrets.

Don't let it worry you, because you can play the game too. Call the man over, and get a price from him. Whatever figure he mentions, brush it aside. No, no, you say. Give me the trade price. (Normally, quite a lot less.)

The dealer will look at you through narrowed eyes. Are you really another dealer, or just a robber in a well-cut suit? You give him a business card and show him your cheque book, and there it is, printed proof: 'COOPER ANTIQUES, PERIOD FURNITURE, VIEWING BY APPOINTMENT ONLY'.

I know a man who has been doing this for years, and he has now completely refurnished his house at special trade prices, even though he's no more a dealer than my butcher's dog is. When I asked him if he thought that this was the kind of sharp practice that an unsporting judge might describe as fraudulent misrepresentation, he just grinned. Didn't I know? Most antiques bounce back and forth between dealers for years before they find places in private homes. All he was doing, in his own small way, was helping to speed up the turnover of stock, giving the dealers the money to go out and buy more antiques from other dealers. The way he saw it, he was doing the entire business a service.

Even if you're not prepared to disguise yourself as a gentleman dealer, you must still resist the impulse to pay the asking price. Make an offer, but not before making a few disparaging remarks about rickety legs, dents, scars and interesting blemishes that have accrued with the passage of centuries. The dealer expects it. In fact, he might be hurt if you didn't point them out, because he may have spent several days in his workshop putting them on.

The process of ageing an object or a piece of furniture overnight – or 'distressing' it – is an art in itself, and it is miraculous what a talented distresser can do with rusty nails and pumice stone and a mixture of soot and beeswax. More miraculous still is how three-legged chairs can suddenly sprout a fourth leg, marquetry with a bad case of acne can regain a smooth complexion and tables originally constructed for midgets can grow to adult height.

Inevitably, some killjoy will try to belittle these marvels of inventive restoration. We all have at least one acquaintance who is a self-appointed expert and whose mission in life is to tell you that you have bought a fake. Shaking his head at your foolishness, he will point out in great detail what you were too dumb to see for yourself. It's not a bad piece, he'll say, but you could hardly call it a genuine antique. But what the hell. Does it matter? If the piece pleases you, if the faking has been done well, who cares? You bought it to live with, not to sell. The antique know-it-all is a pest who should be locked up in the bowels of the Metropolitan Museum to study pre-Columbian bidets.

Occasionally the situation will be reversed and a genuine piece will be treated with as little respect as would a sheet of plywood. I was once in a Manhattan antique shop when a decorator came in with his client. (I knew he was a decorator by the effortless way in which he spent thousands of dollars in the first ten minutes.) He paused in front of a magnificent fifteenth-century oak dining table – absolutely authentic, in wonderful condition, a piece of great rarity. He heard the price without flinching. 'We'll take it,' he said, 'but you'll have to cut two feet off the end so that it will fit in the breakfast alcove.'

The dealer was in shock. I don't like to see a man wrestle with his conscience, so I didn't wait to see whether he sold the table or whether his principles got the better of him. Personally, I like antiques to be used rather than worshipped, but I did wonder how the table's maker would have felt about his work being chopped up and put in a breakfast nook.

Over the years, I have been attracted to a wide variety of antiques, an admirer of all and an expert on none. I have liked Chippendale chairs, Chinese porcelain, kitchen artifacts, Lalique glass, Georgian commodes – just about everything except art, which is a separate and overpriced world of its own. Unfortunately for my aspirations as a collector, I have realised that nature did not equip me for the task. I can't stand living with objects that I have to tiptoe round and hardly dare to touch. I like to be able to sit on chairs, eat at tables, drink from glasses and collapse on to beds without feeling that I am committing sacrilege or risking breakage and financial ruin. I now live with furniture and objects that are either virtually indestructible or easily replaceable. Old, perhaps, but sturdy. I avoid fragility.

And there is something else that I avoid and that, if you are only a moderately rich millionaire, you should avoid too: the chic auction.

The people who go to the big sale rooms, glossy brochures tucked under mink-clad arms, are not like you and me. They might be upper-crust dealers, professional bidders for foundations or just Grade A plutocrats, but they have one thing in common: they are loaded. And when loaded people get together in the over-cranked atmosphere of competitive bidding, prices disappear upwards within seconds. If you should decide, out of curiosity, to be a spectator at one of these million-dollar orgies, the golden rule is to sit on your hands. One absent-minded scratch of your ear might catch the auctioneer's eye and you could find yourself with a twelfth-century bleeding cup and a bill the size of a mortgage. You're safer with Art Nouveau coat-racks.

SERVANTS

I like to have my morning newspaper ironed before I read it. I like to have my shoes boned before they are polished. I like to sit in the back of the car and be driven. I like beds to be made, dishes to be washed, grass to be cut, drinks to be served, telephones to be answered and common tasks to be dealt with invisibly and efficiently so that I can devote my time to major decisions like the choice of wines for dinner and who to vote for in the next election for the mayor of my village.

That is life as it should be lived, and all it takes is money and servants.

The instant and superficial attractions of having a personal staff are such that many a young man has rushed off in search of butlers and maids without pausing first to think the whole thing through. Believe it or not, there are disadvantages that are not immediately apparent. We shall come to those later. But first, the good news.

The most obvious benefit of having servants is that they allow you to avoid disagreeable, uncomfortable or dangerous jobs. They will see to the small but important details of your daily life, from garbage disposal to laying out your clothes every morning and keeping the bar stocked. They can be sent out to do your Christmas shopping, to stand in line outside the movie theatre until you have finished dinner, to open up your house in the country or to lie prone in the street so that you always have a parking space available. If you should stray into an unsavoury neighbourhood, you will have nothing to fear as long as you take a large servant with you. Let him reason with the muggers while you look for a cab.

Aside from practical matters, servants are social assets. They confer status on their master, particularly if they are slightly exotic and don't speak English. My personal preference would be exiled members of the Polish aristocracy. Or you can choose your staff on the basis of their national skills: a French cook (marvellous soufflés), an English valet (wonderful with clothes) and a German chauffeur (mechanically very sound). It all depends on the languages you speak and the size of your establishment.

Here, unfortunately, we begin to come up against the problems of maintaining staff on the premises. Even the smallest servants take up a lot of house room. They must have separate quarters, or you will be forever tripping over the chambermaid in the bedroom or arguing with the butler about which TV programme to watch. In the good old days, servants could be tucked away in the attic, where they polished the silver by the light of a guttering candle, but now the minimum space requirement is a suite of bedroom, bathroom and living room. Obviously, the standard of comfort and decoration will not be anything like your own opulent surroundings. But even so, with rents the way they are, you're looking at an additional overhead of a few thousand dollars a month.

That may not be a problem. Indeed, you may take a benign pleasure in accommodating your servants so well that you hope they will really feel at home. They will. And since no good deed goes unpunished, your generosity will encourage them to behave just like junior members of the family. This inevitably leads to what the English upper classes describe as 'forgetting their place', in other words, a lack of deference that shows itself in many irritating ways: backchat while serving dinner, unflattering remarks about your choice of ties and scotch, overfamiliarity with your guests, demands for longer vacations and all the rest of it.

If you're tolerant enough to put up with this for the sake of a quiet and idle life, worse is to come. Your servants will eventually grow old and develop into eccentrics, like the butler in an Irish country house whose habit it was to serve coffee after dinner stark naked and reeking of Old Bushmills. He was never fired, partly for sentimental reasons and partly because of his close links with the horse-racing fraternity in Dublin, but that's another story.

One final snag: a houseful of servants will lead to an almost total loss of personal privacy. Let us imagine you have had a brutal day at the office. You return home wanting nothing more than a hot tub, a cold bottle of champagne and an hour or so of peaceful reflection while you knit yourself together. Not a chance. As you undress, your valet will be catching your clothes before they hit the floor. You escape to what you hope will be the steamy solitude of the bathroom, only to find one of the maids in there testing the temperature of the water with her elbow and asking if you want your back scrubbed. The butler arrives with the champagne. The valet pops his head through the door to consult you about your plans for the evening so that he can prepare an appropriate outfit, and the chauffeur calls on the bathroom phone to ask when you want the car. The whole damned world is hovering around you, full of concern and good intentions, and it's a nightmare.

With servants, you are never truly on your own, and for some reason they always find something that needs to be done in the room you have chosen for a few moments of quiet rumination. Perhaps it's evidence of effort – an instinctive desire to be seen working – but if you happen to be in the library, it won't be long before someone tiptoes in to dust the bindings. You retire to your study, and they will follow you to change the paper clips. After a while, you will begin to agree with the Spanish proverb that describes servants as 'unavoidable enemies'.

You can, of course, tell them to go away and leave you alone. If you're the sort of man who can kick a cocker spaniel in the teeth without a qualm, you won't be affected by the hurt and reproachful look they give you as they cower out of the room. Otherwise, you will feel guilty and spend the rest of the day being excessively pleasant to them as penance for your harsh behaviour. One way or another, unless you are very careful, the servants you live with will influence your routine and your disposition to such an extent that your life will seem to revolve around them rather than the other way around.

But what are the alternatives? To shine your own shoes, make your own bed, drive your own car and devote your leisure time to drudgery? To be pointed out in the office as the only executive with dishpan hands? To be seen in the supermarket with an armful of toilet-paper rolls? Living with servants might be exasperating, but living without them would be intolerable to a man of your position and refinement.

Do not despair. I have spent many hours thinking about the servant dilemma, and I believe that I have found the solution – an arrangement that gives you privacy when you want it and round-the-clock service when you need it. And, apart from the occasional tip, it won't cost you a cent.

It is a bold and imaginative extension of the corporate lackey system that already exists in every office, the servant hierarchy that starts with cleaners and women who sterilise the phones, progresses through messengers, drivers, maintenance men and secretaries and finally reaches the dizzy level of executive personal assistant. The structure is in place. With some minor adjustments and additions, it can be made to conform precisely to your requirements.

There are only two inflexible rules. The first is that everyone you hire is put on the company payroll. The second is that none of them lives in.

You will need two chauffeurs – one for yourself and one to ferry staff in and out. You will need a cleaner. You will need a housekeeper to supervise general domestic maintenance and a gentleman's gentleman to take care of your wardrobe. Then there is the cook and possibly someone to look after the houseplants and see to it that the flowers are changed every day.

Seven people. What is that to a company? Nothing. When you consider that it is not uncommon for a chairman to have three secretaries, a chauffeur, a pilot for the Lear Jet, a speechwriter and at least one all-purpose minion just to service him during office hours, your retinue looks almost skeletal in comparison. Maybe you should employ a *sommelier* as well to keep your wine cellar up to scratch.

There will be murmurings of dissent, probably from the company treasurer or some busybody in personnel, but their concern will be more with terminology than with principle. 'You can't put a valet on the payroll,' they will say, with the relish of the professional wet blanket. Fair enough. Call him something else – corporate identity adviser, sartorial consultant. As long as it sounds official and businesslike, you will probably get away with it. So the cook will become a home economist, and everyone else can be hidden beneath the impenetrable camouflage of public relations.

And there you have it. Servants when you want them, a home you can call your own, minimal overheads – now that I think of it, this arrangement is one of the very few inducements that might make me consider a return to the office and honest work.

10

IN
DEFENCE
OF
SCROOGE

By its nature, the expensive habit is not only physically gratifying but also beyond the financial reach of all but a fortunate few, thus making it a treat for the ego as well as the body. There is no lasting satisfaction to be gained from eating plover's eggs and wearing four-ply cashmere sweaters if your neighbour, your chauffeur and the urchin who delivers the groceries are all as privileged as yourself. The course of social history is marked by countless expensive habits, from psychoanalysis to travel, that have lost their cachet as they have become more generally available, but man in his ingenuity has always been able to devise rarer and ever more extravagant alternatives to anything that threatens to become commonplace. With one important exception.

Christmas, for some reason, has managed to establish itself as the universal expensive habit, enjoyed (or, more probably, endured) by hundreds of millions of the world's population, most of whom can't afford it. What started as a simple religious celebration has turned into a commercial orgy with a Pentagon-size budget. In the festive build-up, gifts provoke retaliatory gifts. It is a time of year when otherwise sensible and well-adjusted people give serious consideration to the attractions of multilingual speak-your-weight machines, platinum toothpicks, his and hers stress monitors, ostrich-skin desk sets, crushed velvet jogging ensembles, authentic personalised replicas of nineteenth-century spittoons, pens that write underwater, executive egg-timers, bouncing shower soap, luminous bedroom slippers; no excess is so wretched that it doesn't have a chance of being presented to a startled and embarrassed recipient.

The charitable explanation for this frenzied worldwide shopping spree is the inherent generosity of the human spirit, but I have my doubts. I think we have been thoroughly indoctrinated by the erroneous notion that 'tis better to give than to receive, and I attribute most of the blame to a single sinister figure.

He is anonymous, but known to us all. For eleven months a year, we see nothing of him and hope that he might at last have choked on a surfeit of caviare or electrocuted himself with one of his innumerable gadgets. But no. Every December he reappears, venturing out from his thirty-sixth-floor triplex to goad us into near bankruptcy. He is, of course, the Man Who Has Everything.

Why he can't be given a bottle of champagne and a good book and told to stay home and leave us in peace is a mystery that continues to baffle learned men; in any case, if he has everything, why should we humour the acquisitive swine by giving him more? Equally mystifying is why his poverty-stricken but infinitely more deserving cousin, the Man Who Has Nothing, is left to languish in the basement without so much as a pair of hand-monogrammed regimental-striped raw silk undershorts to cheer him up. But then Christmas, like life, is unfair.

Even if you are fortunate enough not to know a Man Who Has Everything, there is still very little chance of being able to greet the New Year in a state of solvency. Being a generous and well organised fellow, you will have planned on giving appropriately thoughtful and expensive gifts to your friends and loved ones, to your secretary, to your kindly old bookmaker and to various other worthy souls who have enriched your life during the past eleven months. Unfortunately, the best laid budgets are invariably put into deficit by the pincer attack that is mounted on your wallet from two directions.

The first is the ambush by faithful retainers. It is quite remarkable how many people, unknown to you throughout the year, have been deeply concerned with your welfare. They begin to come out of the woodwork in early December, heralded by cheery little notes and cards wishing you the compliments of the season and another year of prompt garbage collection, beautifully ironed shirts, safely garaged cars, clean elevators, efficiently patrolled apartment lobbies and trouble-free plumbing. To ignore these hints is to risk having your garbage overlooked, your shirt collars toasted and your fenders crumpled, as well as receiving icy glares from your doorman and having a plumber who is deaf to your cries for help. But at least you won't have to go shopping for these providers of service, because they desire something more personal; something, in fact, that you have made yourself: money.

Less predictable is the attack by the unforeseen gift, an eleventh-hour weapon guaranteed to cause inconvenience as well as expense. It happens when someone with whom you assumed you were merely on Christmas-card terms suddenly escalates the arrangement into the higher and more caring levels of friendship and presents you with a large and affectionately labelled package. No matter that it contains a hammered-pewter jardinière of surpassing ugliness, or that there are only four more shopping hours till Christmas. It's the thought that counts, and if you don't reciprocate, you will spend the entire holiday feeling guilty. And so you abandon your plans for an intimate drink with the blonde in Sales Analysis to brave the stores and join the wild-eyed battalion of last-minute shoppers.

Christmas Eve is without a doubt the worst possible time to make any kind of rational purchase. These are animals with charge cards you're mingling with here – shoving, grabbing, hammering you in the kidneys with gift-wrapped blunt instruments, any semblance of polite behaviour discarded in a stampede of panic buying. Good will to all men! Get out of my way! I saw it first! Trapped in this madhouse, you know you must escape as quickly as you can. You will buy almost anything, and to hell with the expense.

The merchandise director of Santa's Workshop is well aware that this phenomenon takes place on a massive scale every December, and that a normally unsaleable item will be snapped up without a moment's hesitation. That is why you will find such a bizarre selection of goods on display. Surely, you think as you survey the counters in astonishment, no person in his right mind could give stuff like this to a friend. But people can. And they do. And the friend on the receiving end will occasionally be you.

The embarrassing gift can take many different forms, but it is always distinguished by the following characteristics. First, it is something that makes you wince each time you see it – a cushion with a cute motto, for instance, or a large ornament in nightmare colours. It is permanent; that is, you cannot excuse its absence from your living room by saying that you've eaten it, used it up or worn it out. And, worst of all, it is given to you by someone whose feelings you don't want to hurt, who visits you frequently, and whose first act on coming through the door is to check that the unspeakable object is prominently featured in your otherwise impeccably tasteful home. Over the years, you will fill several closets with these horrors, getting them out and dusting them off just before the donors arrive. They, naturally, are touched by the obvious care with which you have looked after their gifts and will make a mental note to give you something similar for your birthday.

Once in a while, though, the unforeseen gift can bring a measure of joy to the most hardened and unfestive of men. I have a friend whose dislike of Christmas is matched only by his profound aversion to his mother-in-law, whose annual visit is the low point of his year. But one Christmas Eve, in addition to the customary necktie, she gave him the flu. It was necessary that he retire to bed, congested but happy, until she left on New Year's Day. He said it was the first time he hadn't wanted to take a gift of hers back and exchange it.

It would be a mistake, however, to think of Christmas purely in commercial terms of dollars and cents and gifts. There are other prices to be paid, as there always are on occasions of enforced jollity, particularly when different generations are thrown together and obliged to have a Wonderful Time. A sociologist has put forward the theory that Christmas is the cause of more family disputes than anything else, with the possible exception of sloppy bathroom habits or adultery, and it is not difficult to see how he arrived as his conclusion.

The classic holiday gathering consists of the children, the parents and the grandparents, an uneasy combination that is complicated by the guest appearances of neighbours and family friends who come by for a drink. The children, who have been up since 5 a.m., have broken their more fragile toys and are bored and ready for lunch by eleven, just about the time when the adults feel they can decently reach for the bottle. The first visitors arrive. Against the background of electronic hiccups from little Billy's zap gun and the programme of carols blaring from the stereo, valiant attempts are made at conversation. The grandparents, unaccustomed to so much noise and alcohol, retreat to the kitchen and, for lack of anything else to do, burn the turkey. The visitors (do you think they *always* drink that much in the morning?) seem set to stay for the day, probably because they know what's waiting for them at home. But eventually they are persuaded to go, and lunch is served.

It is not as Norman Rockwell used to draw it. Little Billy, who has been furtively stuffing himself with candy canes all morning, threatens to be sick. The parents can already feel the first faint twinges of eggnog headaches. The grandparents think longingly of a nap. No such luck. This is a family Christmas, damn it, and we're going to enjoy ourselves, despite first-degree exhaustion, frazzled nerves and the promise of indigestion and afternoon hangovers. Vast reserves of patience and fortitude are required to prevent the day from ending in silent and ill-tempered torpor round the TV.

And there we might leave it, except that Christmas isn't really over until the closing days of January, when, with ghastly inevitability, the bills arrive. As you sit amid the financial wreckage, you think fondly of one of the most underrated figures in literature. Dear old Scrooge, bless him. He would never have allowed you to get into this mess, and he would have just one word for the Man Who Has Everything: bah!

Happy New Year.

11

HOW
THE
RICH
KEEP
WARM

Winters in Mongolia are brisk. The winds howl over the permafrost, jogging is an undiscovered treat and most of the locals need regular tots of rum and hot yak's milk to keep from icing up. It is cold enough to freeze the ear flaps off a fur hat.

There are, however, some native Mongolians who thrive on the sub-zero temperatures. A bracing nip in the air means nothing to them because they are, in effect, walking sweaters. Swathed from nose to hoof in one of nature's most efficient forms of antifreeze, they are perfectly insulated. You will never see a Mongolian cashmere goat shivering.

Pure Mongolian cashmere, generally acknowledged to be the best, is warmer in relation to its weight than is any other natural fibre, and the goat has two layers of it to keep out the draughts. The first is a coarse outer coat of guard hair, the second a much finer coat of underhair. It is this finer hair that will one day take its place in your wardrobe. In addition to its lightness and warmth, it has a softness that is irresistibly tactile and instantly recognisable. You can pick out a cashmere sweater with your eyes closed, simply by using your fingertips.

It is also reassuringly expensive. Ounce for ounce, only vicuña – which comes from a family of privileged camels who live in the mountains of South America – costs more, and there is little chance that the price of cashmere will ever be less than steep. This is partly due to the quality and rarity of the fibre and is partly a result of the mediaeval methods that are still used to get the hair off the goat's back and on the way to yours.

The whole process of turning goat's hair into gentlemen's clothing is inconvenient, labour-intensive and subject to all kinds of imponderables – one of the most imponderable being the sex drive of the suppliers. Cashmere goats cannot be cooped up and made to multiply like battery chickens. Rather like us, they need space and privacy for romance, and it is impossible to predict with any accuracy how much cashmere there will be from year to year. It is a natural commodity, and, like all commodities, its price will fluctuate. More often than not, upward.

It would be easier and cheaper if the goats could be sheared like sheep, but they can't. The fine under hair moults and becomes tangled up in the coarse outer coat. The only way of getting at it is to comb it out by hand, one goat at a time, yielding only a few ounces of hair per goat. First, of course, you have to catch the goat. Already you can see that this is not simple, quick work.

After combing, the untreated cashmere is transported by a variety of ways and means that would give the president of Federal Express nightmares. By yak, by horse, by raft, by sampan, it dawdles down to one of the depots that will ship it overseas. So far, so slow.

At the warehouse, the cashmere is sorted to separate the grey from the brown from the white, a job that sounds straightforward but requires up to five years of training. It is then blended, scoured to remove the grease that has accumulated during its years with its previous owner and de-haired to pick out any strands of the outer coat that have clung to the batch. By the time this has been done, there may be as little as half of the original quantity left, but what wonderfully comforting and extravagant stuff it will be – the raw material for thousand-dollar sports coats and scarves that feel like a warm massage.

All woven cashmere is not created equal, and you will find it in a range of weights and thicknesses that differ according to use. I imagine that it is technically possible to outfit yourself in everything from a cashmere fedora downwards, but there are some practical limitations to consider. Much as I love cashmere, one or two of my experiments with it have taken their toll in money and disappointment.

The idea of cashmere socks, for instance, is altogether delightful, a well-deserved treat for the feet. What could be more pleasant than walking around with your toes cocooned in warm, comfortable money? And pleasant it certainly is. But not for long – or, at least, not for me. It may be that I have unforgiving and abrasive heels or a savage and destructive tread, but I find that a pair of cashmere socks might, if I confine walking to the absolute minimum, last through the day intact. If they do, the next time I wear them they

will undoubtedly develop premature baldness. Either a toe will impudently pop out of the front or a heel will emerge from the back. I have reluctantly decided to abandon cashmere socks.

The problems with trousers are not as extreme or revealing, but similar. Even when fully lined, they have a tendency to bag at the seat and the knees, giving the wearer a slightly droopy lower profile. Short of standing upright all day, the only solution, if you're determined to have some form of cashmere covering your bottom half, is to choose a blend of cashmere and wool or cashmere and silk. It's not quite as soft, to be sure, but it is more likely to stay in shape.

Your upper half is where you can indulge yourself with more layers than a goat's. A cashmere overcoat, with its dense nap and its texture somewhere between velvet and fur, is proof against the Madison Avenue wind-chill factor and the Eskimo winters of Minnesota but without the heaviness of clumsier overcoats that make you feel as though you're wearing your grandmother's armchair. And, as your tailor will tell you, cashmere is a joy to cut.

Peeling off your outer layer, we come to your sports coat, where warmth is less important than is appearance. Practised cashmere spotters – and it doesn't take long to become one – can tell a pure cashmere sports coat from ten feet away. Even at that distance, it is visibly soft. There are no hard edges. Women, who have an instinctive eye for these things, often have great difficulty keeping their hands to themselves when a cashmere sports coat comes within touching distance. If you wear cashmere, you must be prepared to be stroked from time to time. There are worse fates in life.

For all but the most cold-blooded, that should be enough cashmere to have on at any one time, although there are sweaters fine enough to wear under a sports coat. These are single-ply, which is the most widely used weight. Two-ply is twice as heavy, twice as warm, nearly twice as expensive. And for the sweater of sweaters, the one you will keep under lock and key, well away from light-fingered women, there is four-ply.

I have a weakness for four-ply cashmere sweaters, a terrible weakness that I try to justify on the feeble grounds that I rarely wear a sports coat. In fact, it would be impossible to wear a sports coat that wasn't cut like a marquee, because four-ply cashmere is so warm, so lush and so preposterously thick that wearing anything over it is out of the question. It is worth ten ordinary sweaters – and costs about the same as all ten put together. (For those of you who doubt the wisdom of plunging immediately into a sweater investment of such daunting proportions, I can recommend the four-ply cashmere scarf. Wrap it round your neck and get out in the coldest weather you can find. The rest of you may turn blue, but from chin to chest you won't feel anything but snug.)

Now that demand for the cosy pleasures of cashmere is increasing, it is becoming more widely available: every good men's shop (particularly the kind that describes itself as a 'purveyor of gentleman's furnishings') will have a selection, displayed under glass, in the high-rent corner of the store. But sooner or later, if you take your cashmere seriously, you and your American Express card will have to make a pilgrimage to London and investigate the temptations of the Burlington Arcade.

It runs at right angles off Piccadilly, about 250 yards long and barely wider than a couple of scarves laid end to end, with a glass roof and immaculately buffed display windows. It is patrolled by beadles, resplendent in a kind of Ruritanian policeman's uniform, whose job is to keep the peace and enforce the gentlemanly regulations that preserve the dignity of the arcade: no whistling and no running.

In this short but opulent alley, you will see cashmere in a glorious, luxurious glut, piled up in the windows and on the counters, any colour you want, any thickness you can afford. The territory is divided among four principal retailers, the cashmere barons – Berk, Fisher, Lord and Peal – each of whom offers his own variations on the classic styles. Prices differ a little – but nothing to get excited about. Cut-rate cashmere doesn't exist.

The only time you might find a glimmer of a bargain is during cashmere's off-season, during what is optimistically referred to in Britain as high summer. In August, if you're lucky, there might just be a certain amount of restrained stock clearing – nothing as vulgar as an everything-must-go sale, but a distinctly more sympathetic look to the price tags. August is the time of year I buy sweaters, and Mr Fisher is the man I go to see. I like the styles he has, and I like him.

This year, his news was not good. The price of untreated cashmere, straight off the goat, is nudging £300 a kilo. A four-ply sweater, weighing in at just over half a kilo, leaves very little change from £550. Next year's prices could be higher still, but what can you do if those damned goats won't perform?

12

A MOUTHFUL OF BLACK PEARLS

Very few single words in the English language are instantly evocative of wealth, privilege and a taste of bliss all at once. (Phrases don't count – not even 'oysters Rockefeller' or 'Peel me a grape.') It is a select gathering, a verbal hall of fame, and one of the oldest established and least likely members is the oily, processed fish egg.

Caviare. You see? The very mention of the word has you mentally rubbing shoulders with the rich and knees with the beautiful as you sample the most consistently popular luxury food in the world. Caviare has been receiving superb reviews for more than 2,000 years. Aristotle wrote about it in the fourth century BC, and writers have been salivating in print ever since, from Rabelais and Shakespeare to Evelyn Waugh and every cookery expert who has that redeeming streak of extravagance that saves us from a life filled with meat-loaf recipes.

Unlike many ancient titbits – larks' tongues, flamingo brains, roasted swan, peacock breasts and dozens of other dishes that have become extinct as a result of changing tastes or changing laws – caviare has survived to be with us still. Not with many of us, it's true, but then if it were as available and inexpensive as spareribs or hamburger, half the pleasure of eating it would be lost: an order of caviare on a sesame-seed bun, hold the relish, is somehow lacking in cachet and would certainly take away from the delightful, almost guilty feeling of elitism that adds so much to the enjoyment of every slippery spoonful.

A great deal of what is optimistically classified as caviare is, strictly speaking, nothing of the sort. It may be processed fish roe and it may have an agreeable taste, but it will have come from lumpfish, salmon, white fish, cod or one of several other pregnant members of the fish family. In the United States, as long as the name of the parent fish appears somewhere on the can or jar, the processed roe can be sold as caviare. In France, where matters of the stomach are treated with the utmost gravity, the definition of caviare is as precise and rigorously enforced as the definition of champagne: only the roe of the sturgeon qualifies as caviare.

Fate and man have not been kind to the sturgeon. Until the turn of the century, it was still swimming in the Hudson River and in rivers throughout Europe. Since then, overfishing and pollution have practically wiped it out, and with a few isolated exceptions, the only bodies of water where it is still found in significant numbers are the Caspian and Black Seas and the Gironde River in France. And to add to the sturgeon's misfortunes, the Caspian Sea is shrinking. (The Russians, who eat more caviare than anyone else, are trying to do something about it, but refilling a sea is a lengthy business.)

Of the surviving sturgeon, the two best known are the beluga and the sevruga – the largest and smallest members of the species and the names to look for when you're feeling sufficiently prosperous. The beluga can reach a length of fifteen feet and weigh over a thousand pounds, and twenty per cent or more of its body weight can be made up of roe. Beluga eggs are the largest and are a long time in the making; it takes twenty years before the female is mature enough to produce them. The sevruga weight in at about fifty pounds, matures in seven years and produces the smallest eggs.

If it were enough simply to catch the sturgeon and extract the eggs, caviare would be considerably less expensive, but it would taste nothing like it does. Roe, even sturgeon roe, is fairly bland stuff. What transforms it into caviare is the way it is processed, and that takes enough dexterity and knowledge to justify calling it an art.

More than a dozen separate operations have to be carried out within the space of about fifteen minutes: any longer, and the roe will deteriorate beyond the stage at which it can be made into caviare. First, the sturgeon is knocked out – not killed, as this would make the deterioration take place even faster – and then the eggs are removed, sieved, washed and drained to prepare them for the attentions of one of those mythical figures who, like great wine makers, can improve dramatically on nature's raw materials.

The grader, or taster, or, as he should properly be called, the master of caviare, has literally minutes to make decisions that will determine the taste and the price of the eggs heaped in front of him. He sniffs, he tastes, he looks, he feels with the tips of his fingers. He grades the eggs according to size, colour, firmness, bouquet and flavour, and finally makes the most important decision of all: how much, or how little, salt is needed to ripen the roe into caviare without overpowering the subtle combination of taste and texture.

The highest-quality eggs receive the minimum amount of salt, less than five per cent in relation to the amount of roe, and can be described as malossol caviare. (Malossol means 'little salt' in Russian but can mean considerably more than a little in the USA, where, once again, the laws of description are less stringent.) After salting, the eggs are shaken on sieves until dry and packed in cans that are small enough – two kilos, or just over four pounds – to prevent the weight of the eggs on top from bursting those on the bottom. And then the caviare starts its refrigerated journey from the Caspian Sea to the small number of favoured establishments around the world whose clients can afford to pay $5 or more a mouthful.

In fact, when you consider the scarcity of sturgeon, the years it takes for the female to produce her eggs, the enormous skill required for processing and the difficulties of transportation, it is easy to see why caviare is one of the three most expensive edible items in the world (saffron and truffles being the other two). Looked at in terms of dollars and ounces, it should be given the serious consideration of a major investment, the difference being that this will taste better than your holdings in IBM or the Monet hanging in your bedroom.

As with anything natural, delicate and perishable, it is critically important to find a supplier you can trust, and one who sells enough caviare to take the trouble to store it properly. There are no special offers on caviare and it always pays to buy from the best houses, such as Petrossian in New York or Fortnum's in London. Providing you look like a genuine purchaser and not someone in search of a quick snack, you might be allowed to taste before you buy. Ironically, the suppliers who are confident enough about their caviare to offer this pleasant service are the ones whose advice you can trust without the free trial.

Buy only as much as you're going to eat, and once you've bought the caviare, don't go back to the office, drop into a bar or dawdle through the park to look at the girls. Go straight home and put your caviare in the fridge. In its sealed container, it will keep for about four weeks. Once opened, it will, in theory, keep for a couple of days; in practice, however, there are never any leftovers.

You now have to make a series of choices. They may seem small, but they will make the difference between your caviare being the treat it should be or an expensive disappointment, and at the top of the list is your choice of companion.

Some people can be ruled out at once. Gastronomic philistines who have ketchup with everything are best left to wallow in their vice at a hot-dog stand. Your boss and your friendly IRS inspector should be excluded because they will both assume you're making far too much money. Business contacts will think you're trying to impress them, and will eat more than their fair share. Relatives don't deserve it. The choices narrow down to an intimate friend, or the one person in life you love above all others, who is, of course, yourself. Dinner for one when caviare is on the menu is a dinner you will remember.

And what should you drink with it? The tradition is Russian or Polish vodka, the bottle frozen in a block of ice so that the vokda is so cold it stings. But don't be tempted to experiment with the flavoured vodkas: they will fight with the taste of the caviare and usually win. Personally, I prefer a very dry champagne. There is something nicely symmetrical about not only eating bubbles but drinking them as well.

The preparation and serving of the caviare itself is often absurdly complicated. You will frequently see people piling their plates with ingredients that will either disguise or obliterate the very flavour they have paid for so dearly in the first place. On go the dollops of sour cream, the slivers of anchovy, the chopped capers and onion and hard-boiled eggs, and what are you left with? It might taste good, but it won't taste of caviare.

The best way to eat caviare is the simplest way: straight. If you're going to eat it from a plate, chill the plate. If you're going to eat it from the container, put the can or jar in a bed of crushed ice. Thin toast with unsalted butter, blinis or a drop or two of lemon juice are optional, but there are no options when it comes to the method of transport that will take the caviare on the last leg of its journey into your mouth. It has to be a spoon.

You will see people – very often the same people who smother their caviare with irrelevancies like chopped onion and egg – using a knife to grind the mixture on to a piece of toast as though they were making a peanut-butter sandwich. They are vandals. The whole point of caviare, the reason it is so difficult and expensive to process and ship, is that the eggs must arrive in your mouth unbroken. Only then, as you crush them between your tongue and your palate, do you experience that tiny savoury explosion that all the fuss is about. If the eggs have already been broken by the pressure of a knife, the high point of a mouthful of caviare has taken place on the toast instead of on your tongue. So it has to be a spoon.

Caviare addicts will debate the respective merits of spoons with the passion that is common to many participants in life's arcane little rituals. Strangely enough, the spoon that all fortunate babies have in their mouths at birth – the silver spoon – is one to avoid, as it can impart a slightly metallic taste. Otherwise, take your pick: gold, ivory, wood, mother-of-pearl, horn or – my favourites – those short plastic spoons you can get in handfuls from the deli. They are easy to manage, they are soft and have no sharp edges that might puncture the eggs, they are functional, hygienic and disposable. They have no after taste, and they are often free. I recommend them.

Your final decision is where and when to spoil yourself, and here you will begin to appreciate one of the less obvious virtues of caviare. It is, in the best sense of the word, a convenience food. You can eat it in bed without having to go through any dangerous contortions with knife and fork. You can eat it in the back of your limousine as you come home from the office (a one-ounce jar, consumed slowly, as it should be, with pauses for drink and contemplation, will last you from Wall Street to Park Avenue).

You can eat it sitting on the floor in front of a log fire, or while relaxing in a warm bath. It doesn't need an elaborate table setting or a thousand-dollar dinner jacket. Caviare does itself justice without any trimmings.

It is a food for good times and bad times, a reward for triumphs and a consolation for disasters. It will taste wonderful on the day you make your first million, and maybe even better as a final defiant gesture before backruptcy; at the beginning of a love affair, or at the end. There is always an excuse for caviare, and if you can't immediately think of one, you can eat it simply for reasons of health. There is a rumour that caviare is good for you.

At seventy-four calories an ounce, it would cost you tens of thousands of dollars before you started putting on weight. Caviare is reputed to be an aphrodisiac, a remedy for hangovers and a restorative for overtaxed livers. It contains forty-seven minerals and vitamins, and the female sturgeon's only mistake in producing an otherwise faultless delicacy is that the sodium count is a little high. But what the hell. Nobody's perfect.

13

THE PERFECT SECOND HOME

I used to see him all over the world, and I envied him. He would turn up in Geneva and Nassau, in Nice and Ibiza, always recognisable, even though I only ever caught a glimpse of him, and usually from a distance. I never met him; our paths crossed only at airports. But I could pick him out from fifty yards away, and from among hundreds of other travellers. While the rest of us were struggling with ungainly bundles of vacation paraphernalia – the ski boots, the tennis racquets, the fishing rods, the scuba-diving equipment, the overstuffed carry-on bags – and waiting to claim our freshly mutilated suitcases, I would see him strolling through customs with nothing more to weigh him down than a magazine and a couple of books. He didn't need anything else. It was all waiting for him there, in his ski lodge or beach house. He was the man with the second home.

In theory, the second home makes sense. It is always available. It is in a desirable part of the world, where real-estate prices should appreciate steadily over the years. Lying in the sun or swooping down the piste, you can tell yourself that you've made a prudent investment. Sitting on your asset, you could even argue that its increasing value is effectively giving you free vacations. And there are fringe benefits: the knowledge that you can take off at a moment's notice with just your passport, the feeling that you are not a mere gawping visitor but a kind of honorary native, the unworthy but pleasing tingle of status that is conferred by mentioning your little place in Antigua or Val d'Isère. Not for you the twenty-one-day all-inclusive package that the rest of humanity has to endure. You are the man apart, the man with a foreign front-door key.

That's how it used to seem to me, and when I started to meet people who had second homes, I would ask them to tell me how wonderful it all was. I became the vicarious owner, at one time or another, of a house in Jamaica's Port Antonio, an apartment in Gstaad, a studio in Paris, a farmhouse in Tuscany and a boat in Key West. The collected wisdom and experience of the various proprietors saved me a fortune and cured me forever. I don't want to own a second home. I haven't got the stamina.

To start with, there are the simple things, like books and music and clothes. Where are you going to keep them – in your home, or in your home away from home? Or are you going to duplicate everything? If you don't, one of the immutable laws of nature will come into play, and you will find that the books you really want to read, the records you want to listen to, the old and well-loved silk shirts – they're all thousands of miles away. It's a small problem, nothing that money and a Teutonic flair for detailed organisation can't overcome, but that's only the beginning.

Assuming that you will want to escape for a few carefree days in your second home whenever you feel like it, you won't rent it out. Consequently, it will remain empty for weeks or months on end, and so the first few days of every visit will be spent getting supplies in, attending to minor repairs and generally making the place comfortable in time for your departure. That's if you're lucky. It can be much worse.

My friends with the Tuscan farmhouse arrived one year for their rural Christmas idyll to find the driveway to their house sealed off. A local peasant had decided that it crossed a small part of his land and had blocked it with chains and concrete. It was a 300-yard walk through the mud up to the house, and waiting in the mailbox was notification of the lawsuit that the peasant was bringing against them.

The owner of the studio in Paris went over for a week in the spring with the girl of his dreams and, for one horrible moment, thought that someone had died in the bathroom. It was worse. A pipe had burst, and the waste from the upstairs apartment had been building up for weeks all over the floor. He was never again able to feel that old sweet nostalgia for April in Paris without thinking of plumbing.

Over in Jamaica, our man in Port Antonio discovered that his house wasn't as empty as he had thought. A family of bush rats – quite a large family, from the sound of it – had moved in and made themselves thoroughly at home. The bush rat is not a fussy eater and, if undisturbed, will experiment with all kinds of new tastes.

In this case, the menu had included rattan furniture, soap, candles, rugs and half a mattress.

Of course, you will say, all these surprises can be avoided by hiring a caretaker, some trusty soul who will look after your second home as if it were his own. Alas, he may become so attached to it that he will bring a moving van and take all the contents to where he can keep a closer eye on them, as happened to some friends in Spain. But most caretakers won't go that far. I'm told that they are usually quite happy to drop by every day to take care of what's left of the liquor supply and make long-distance phone calls.

I am not by nature a pessimist, but after listening to stories like these I found that my enthusiasm for owning a second home had been replaced by relief that my problems didn't include bush rats and larcenous caretakers. I was, however, still enthusiastic about the idea of having somewhere else to go every year. Pot-luck vacations didn't appeal to me. Nor did time-sharing. And I have never liked imposing myself on friends for extended stays ('Fish and guests smell at three days old' is a Danish proverb that puts it succinctly). What I wanted were the advantages of a second home – the familiar, but different surroundings – without any of the horrors of ownership or the chores of the part-time proprietor. I think I've found the answer, although it will be another year or two before I know for sure. In the meantime, research and field tests continue.

The idea is simple, and it works like this: With a map of the world in one hand and a list of your leisure preferences in the other, pick a spot that has the basic facilities you want – tennis, windsurfing, girls, whatever it is that will sustain your interest in the years to come. The next essential is the matter of creature comforts, and now that the tentacles of civilisation are so wide-spread, these are not as difficult to find as you might think. Whether your idea of heaven is skiing in Australia or salmon-fishing in the Scottish Highlands, you can be sure that someone has got there ahead of you and opened a luxury hotel. Go and stay in it.

On your first visit, look the place over with the eye of a pro-spective investor rather than a transient guest. If you like what you see, and you think that you will continue to like it, make yourself known to the manager and tell him that you intend to become his most faithful and regular client. Have him show you a selection of the best rooms and suites. Choose one, and ask him to give you a price based on a series of guaranteed reservations spread over the next three to five years. He may or may not offer you a deal, but that hardly matters to a man of your means, because what you will gain by this arrangement is more important than a few dollars' discount; what you will gain is special treatment.

First of all, you will be known, unlike the multitudes of other guests who pass through the hotel each year. With some early and judicious tipping, you will not only be known but deeply loved. Your suite will always be ready for you, your little idiosyncrasies will be catered to, your mail will be held for you, the barman will know what you like to drink, your place by the pool and in the restaurant will be assured – you will, in other words, be spoiled. There is only one slight inconvenience to be dealt with, and that is your vacation equipment. It is tiresome and unnecessary to keep coming and going laden down with skis or spear-fishing guns or mountaineering boots. How much simpler life would be if they were kept at the hotel. And while you're at it, why not leave a selection of clothes there as well? Your new friend, the manager, will be happy to perform this small service for such a valued and consistent guest, and then your bag-carrying days will be over. You will be traveling light, just like the man I used to envy.

Once this has been arranged, you will have achieved the perfect second home. It will be familiar and extremely comfortable. You won't be involved in any of the dreary operational details like making beds or shopping for groceries. You will be immune from ghastly surprises. Friends can come and stay without disturbing you in any way (they won't mind having accommodation slightly inferior to yours as long as you entertain them in your suite occasionally), and your vacations will be what they should be – that is, a considerable improvement on real life.

The cost of having a second home with a staff of 150 and all the small attentions a modest man could want will vary enormously, depending on the number of visits each year and the distance from your principal home. It will either be expensive, or very expensive, and will certainly not be less than £200 a day, although against this you can obviously offset the cost of a normal vacation. But that's almost incidental. The real question is whether it makes sense to toss your money around in this delightful fashion instead of buying a place of your own, and here I can only offer my own experience and conclusions.

I live in southern France, and go to London or Paris several times a year. At one time I thought about buying an apartment in London – nothing palatial, just a humble place where I could keep my suits and lay my head for two or three weeks a year. But after a morning with real-estate agents, I gave up, because the initial cost of a small apartment in a pleasant area of central London is now around £120,000. On top of that, there are the annual property taxes, the building maintenance charges and the household costs, all of which add up to maybe £5,000 a year.

For £5,000, I can stay in one of my favourite hotels, the Connaught, for two or three weeks a year. I can leave my shoes to be shined every night while I sleep, I can eat in the best hotel restaurant in London, I can have chambermaids and bartenders and concierges dancing attendance, and my tailor is just across the street. If I were to spend the price of an apartment – £120,000 – on these excursions, I could stay at the Connaught every year for the next twenty-five years. With a bit of luck, I might even manage to die there after a particularly good dinner, content in the knowledge that my corpse would be disposed of in a discreet and tasteful manner. The service there is marvellous.

14

THE
TRUE
CIGAR

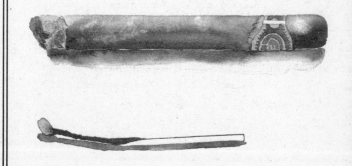

S moking is now considered to be such a noxious and anti-social habit that anyone who has a good word to say about tobacco risks being beaten round the ears with a rolled-up copy of the latest surgeon general's report. The cigarette has been condemned as a villain. To a certain extent, its longer, fatter, deep-brown cousin has also been brushed by the same tar, and this is unfair. Smoking a cigar is altogether different from dragging on a cigarette: the smoke is not inhaled, and therefore the body is not affected in the same way; the absorption of nicotine and other substances is infinitely less. Yet the enjoyment, for the man who knows how to treat a cigar, is infinitely greater. It is the difference between a sandwich at your desk and lunch at Lutèce.

Of course, it has to be a true cigar. We are not concerned here with those small mud-coloured tubes wrapped in recycled paper, coated with syrup and tipped with a plastic appendage. These may be called cigars, but they bear little resemblance to the real thing, and we shall leave them in decent obscurity, where they belong, on the candy-store shelf.

Good cigars come from several parts of the world. Brazil, Mexico, Jamaica and Holland, for example, all produce a respect-able selection, varying in length and strength from the little Dutch Schimmelpennincks to the more impressively sized Jamaican Macanudos. But as worthy and well made as these undoubtedly are, there is no real argument about where the best cigars come from, and that is Cuba – home of the *puro*. The writer Bernard Wolfe has described the whole island as a natural humidor; no other place on earth possesses that special and precise combination of soil, sun, wind and water that is so perfectly suited to the cultivation of tobacco. And that is why no other place on earth breeds a cigar that looks, feels, smells and tastes as satisfying as a genuine Havana. Unfortunately, that holdover from the JFK days, the ban on Cuban trade, has rendered Havanas hard to come by in the United States – you'll have to leave the country to buy them legally; but it's a worthwhile excursion.

Even before you come to grips with the cigar itself, there are small pleasures to be enjoyed, starting with the box – an ornately decorated yet functional relic from the days before the invention of plastic. A true cigar box is made from cedarwood, which allows the tobacco to breathe and to continue maturing. It is sealed with what looks like a high-denomination bank note (the export warranty of the respective government), and it is often covered with the kind of baroque graphic art that conjures up thoughts of brandy and boudoirs: curlicues, gold embossing, vignettes of white-bosomed ladies and bewhiskered gentlemen, florid typography – everything, in fact, that nineteenth-century pop artists could lay their hands on.

When you open the box, your nose is treated to a classic aroma, a bouquet that deserves a few quiet moments of appreciation before you proceed any further. It is a particularly masculine scent, and men have been known to line their clothes closets with the thin leaves of cedarwood that separate the fat rows of cigars. (The thought of walking around smelling like a human corona may not appeal to all of us, but there are, God knows, worse things to smell of, as anyone who has been ambushed and sprayed on his way through the cosmetics department at Bloomingdale's will confirm.)

Now we come to the cigars, looking as prosperous and well filled as a group of investment bankers after a killing. This is the beginning of what should be at least forty-five minutes of unhurried enjoyment. Cigars should never be rushed, or puffed absentmindedly while you're doing deals on the phone. The more attention you give them, the more pleasure they will give you, so if you don't have a quiet hour or so, save the cigar until later. The leisurely ceremonial of preparing and smoking one of nature's minor triumphs is worth the investment in time.

A knowledgeable smoker will always inspect his cigar before committing himself. This is not an affectation; good cigars are made by human hands, which are fallible, and are sometimes stored in unsuitable conditions, which can be fatal. A cigar in its prime will feel firm as you roll it between thumb and index finger, and slightly elastic as you squeeze it. Brittle cigars will not taste good, and should be put aside for less discriminating smokers, such as politicians.

If the cigar pleases your eye, your nose and your fingers, the next step is to make an incision in the wrapper at the head so that the smoke can be drawn through. Surgical techniques vary from smoker to smoker. Rambo, should he ever do anything as un-American as smoke a Cuban cigar, would probably bite off the end. More delicate souls will use a cigar cutter or even a sharp fingernail to make a small opening. The cut should be clean, and not too deep; if you stab a cigar in the head with a penknife or a toothpick, you will create a funnel, which results in a hot, bitter smoke.

The last stage before lighting up is optional. Should you remove the band – that miniature work of art just below the head – or should you leave it on? When it was first invented (credit is often given to Gustave Bock, a Dutchman), the band had a practical purpose, which was to prevent the outer wrapper from coming adrift as the cigar heated up. Nowadays, with more reliable gumming methods, the risk of losing the wrapper is very slight, so it comes down to a question of aesthetics. Do you prefer your cigars to be decorated or totally nude? Either is fine, and only pedants make a fuss about it.

So you've rolled and you've squeezed and you've sniffed and you've cut, and now you are ready to light up. Once again, a certain finesse is required, and certain laws of nature should be observed. The most important rule is never to use a petrol lighter unless you like the taste of petrol fumes. Similarly, don't be tempted to lean across the dinner table and gaze into the décolletage of your beloved as you light up from a candle. Wax and tobacco don't mix. Use a match. When you have the cigar in your mouth, bring the flame close to the end (about one third of an inch away) and rotate it so that you make an even burn that starts at the rim and spreads to the centre.

You can now settle back and take the first luxurious puff. There is a richness of texture to cigar smoke that makes inhaling quite unnecessary: it is enough just to hold the smoke in the mouth for a few seconds before blowing it gently toward the heavens. And as you watch it hanging in the air, thick and blue-grey and aromatic, you can easily imagine that what you are smoking was hand-rolled on a Cuban maiden's long brown thigh. (I doubt that this delightful practice still exists in the cigar factories, but a man can dream.)

'The cigar smoker,' wrote Marc Alyn, 'is a calm man, slow and sure of his wind.' You will never see an experienced cigar man taking quick, agitated puffs. He is concentrating – albeit in a relaxed and sometimes even trance-like fashion – on the pleasure of the moment. This mood of leisurely well-being that is induced by a good cigar is perhaps its greatest attraction. It even has social benefits, because this mild euphoria makes heated argument almost impossible. Nobody but a clod would waste a £25 Havana by waggling it around for emphasis or stubbing it out in anger.

Despite a good cigar's tranquillising effect, it doesn't kill conversation. Quite the contrary, since it encourages contented and appreciative listeners. (Why do you think cigars are handed out at the end of formal dinners? Obviously, to render the audience benign, no matter how long and terrible the speeches are.) Stories told over a cigar are funnier, observations are more profound, pauses are comfortable, the cognac is smoother, and life is generally rosier. An hour with a good cigar and a couple of friends is a vacation from life's nonsense.

Of course, there is a right way and a wrong way to wear cigars, and anyone serious about them will do well to observe the following rules:

- We have all seen short men with small faces trying unsuccessfully to look at ease with a cigar that is several sizes too big for them. It doesn't work. Choose a cigar that fits your face, from the small panatella (about four and a half inches long) to the double corona (between eight and nine inches). The regular corona, at five and a quarter inches, is probably the best bet for anyone with a conventionally sized face.
- Don't keep a cigar in your mouth. It makes speech difficult and the end wet.
- There is no need to invest in a cigar holder. Smoking a Havana through a holder is a disappointing experience, rather like drinking good claret from a Styrofoam cup.
- Although King Edward VII is supposed to have said that the

way to deal with a cigar was to pierce it with a lance, light it and wave it in the air, it is best to avoid grand gestures. You will lose the ash prematurely and constitute a fire hazard to your companions.

The cost of cigar-induced pleasure will obviously depend on how often and how seriously you take it. If all you want is an occasional treat, it's best to buy your cigars one at a time from a reputable merchant. It doesn't make sense to buy a box if you anticipate smoking a mere half a dozen cigars a year, because dry heat or air-conditioning will spoil the rest. Annual expenditure, therefore, is unlikely to be more than about £100. A regular smoker, however, can easily spend this much in a week, and a passionate smoker will have to add on the price of board and lodging. Good cigars need to be kept as carefully as good wines.

The climate preferred by cigars is warm – between 65 and 75 degrees – with a humidity of 75 per cent. Few of us live permanently in these conditions, so they have to be artificially maintained in a humidor. There are, it's true, simple and inexpensive humidors that will do a perfectly adequate job tucked away in a corner of your living room. But sooner or later reports will reach you of a cigar Utopia, where the conditions are not just adequate but perfect. Needless to say, the inconvenience and extra costs involved in keeping your cigars in such a place add substantially to their appeal. And so you find yourself going to one of the great cigar houses, such as Dunhill in New York, to reserve space in a humidor room.

Not only will your private stock be kept in the best possible conditions outside of Cuba, but you will have the immense satisfaction, when that young smart-ass in the next office wants to show you his new Porsche, of excusing yourself as follows: 'I'm sorry,' you say, 'but I have to go and visit my cigars.'

HOUSE
GUESTS

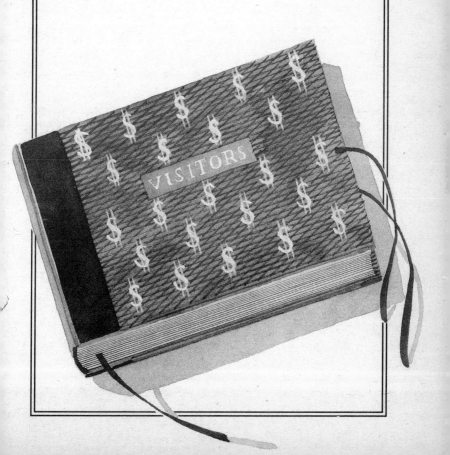

My wife is incurably hospitable, and we live in Provence. This is a disastrous combination if, like me, you feel the occasional need for solitude and regular hours, an orderly life, time to read and all the other advantages of burying yourself in the country. I have found that burial doesn't work. Someone is always arriving to exhume me.

When we first moved here, we were given a prophecy of things to come in the form of a visitors' book. It is becoming dog-eared and wine-stained, its pages filled with often incoherent remarks about the plumbing, the food and the general level of service and customer satisfaction. I looked through the book at the end of last year. Between the beginning of October and Christmas, we had the house to ourselves for a total of ten days. Ten days without guests, and that was our off-peak, out-of-season period. I can't begin to describe what the pages from the summer months look like.

This is not a complaint, but I hope it will serve to establish my credentials as someone who is qualified, or maybe even over-qualified, to comment on the joys of sharing your home with a procession of visitors. No doubt there are lessons to be learned here, even if you live in a fourth-floor walk-up with only a couch to offer in the way of accommodation.

When guests occupy a large part of daily life, there is every reason to include them in the domestic budget along with the other regular expenses, such as liquor and laundry. And naturally, when you consider the guest as an item of expenditure, it is difficult to avoid applying the same criteria that you would to any significant investment, such as a car. So you begin to look at servicing costs, miles per gallon (of wine) and value for money, as well as more technical details like the ability to start in the morning. These will vary; all guests are not created equal.

At the top of the list, underscored in red and marked with a health warning, is the guest who is bound to you by ties of blood, with a permanent claim on your spare room and visiting rights to your most comfortable chair, the cigars you were saving for

Christmas and your stock of malt whisky. It is, of course, that privileged figure, the Relative, who might be an impoverished cousin from Arkansas, a sporting uncle on the run from his bookie, a mother-in-law, a recently divorced brother – the precise form of the relationship doesn't matter, because the behavioural pattern is always the same. It must have something to do with genes.

Relatives don't arrive at your home; they invade it. They kick off their shoes and unpack expansively all over the living-room floor. They pounce on your phone as though they have been starved of contact with the outside world. They have selective vision that excludes dirty dishes and empty bottles. And yet ... all must be forgiven. They're family, and you can be sure that they will never understay their welcome. (Even if they might occasionally mutter about treating the place like a hotel, God forbid you should be so tactless as to mention a check-out time.) Experienced and cunning as I like to think I am, I've never found an effective method of keeping a determined relative at bay. The only sure defence is to be an orphan.

But it would be unkind to suggest that all relatives automatically qualify for the Worst Guest Award. There are many other contenders, and we have had our fair share of them over the years. While new and ingenious refinements in guest performance will probably surprise us in the months to come, the selection that follows represents the worst that we have so far encountered. Names have been withheld to protect the guilty. Potential hosts, be warned: what has arrived on our doorstep could one day arrive on yours.

The waifs

The phone rings, usually in the late afternoon. The caller and his companion have found themselves stranded without hotel reservations. Who would have thought that in mid-August a room would be so difficult to find? Fortunately, they are not far from our house. Would it be possible to squeeze them in just for the night? The night turns into two nights, and then a week, because every hotel for fifty miles is booked solid, the way hotels always are in August.

The indispensable executive

Within minutes of coming through the door, he is on the phone to his office in London. He's been away from his desk for all of five hours, but God knows what might have happened – a management reshuffle engineered by the mail-room boy, a client in distress, the empire crumbling without the emperor. He spends his vacation with our phone sprouting from his ear, stopping only to eat and drink. He talks endlessly about work and is reluctant to leave the house because we don't have an answering machine.

The man with the indestructible bank note

He carries no small change. All he has is this 500-franc note, which is equivalent to about £50, and you won't get that sort of money changed when you're just buying a newspaper or a packet of cigarettes or a couple of beers. So the bank note is taken out and given an airing, apologies are made for not having anything smaller, and someone else pays. It's only a few francs. Anyway, we're all going out to dinner, and restaurants are very happy to take 500-franc notes. But our man has left his cash at home and brought his credit cards, which the restaurant doesn't accept. He promises to settle up later and orders a large cognac. The day of reckoning is postponed by a variety of manoeuvres, and the 500-franc note remains intact.

The virus victims

For the first two or three days they have a wonderful time. They eat, they drink, they take the sun, and then they start to drop like flies. It must have been something in the *salade niçoise* that gave them a stomach bug. They retire to bed and call feebly for beef tea, refusing to admit that the virus is nothing more than their digestive systems' rebelling against the enormous and unac-customed quantities of pink wine that they have been drinking with such enthusiasm. The doctor comes and prescribes suppositories and abstinence, but recovery is gradual. They leave thinner and more pallid than when they arrived.

The open-ended lunch experts

'We thought you wouldn't mind,' they say as they arrive, 'if we brought our friends.' Lunch for four becomes lunch for six. It is quickly apparent that we have been chosen to divert them for the entire afternoon and beyond, because they tell us that they have no further plans for the day. They borrow swim-suits and settle themselves by the pool, and they leave with some disappointment at seven o'clock when it dawns on them that dinner was not included in the lunch invitation.

All visitors, even the most charming and well-behaved ones, cost money; not vast amounts if you take them individually, but enough collectively to make them our single biggest annual expense. There is also a hidden cost, impossible to calculate, and that is exhaustion.

The greatest problem with guests – apart from the indispensable executive – is simple and insoluble: they're on vacation, and we're not. We get up at seven, and I'm at my desk well before nine. They will sleep in, as people on vacation do, until ten or eleven and have a leisurely breakfast in the sun. An hour or so by the pool, and they're ready for a drink and lunch. We go back to work and they go back to reading and sunbathing. Refreshed by a nap in the hammock under the pine trees, they come to life in the evening, moving into high social gear as my wife and I are falling asleep in the soup. And will they go to bed? Not on your life. Not while the night is young and the wine is flowing.

In theory, the one day of the week when we can all lie in and keep the same hours is Sunday, but every guest we have ever had wants to go to one of the big Sunday markets, which start early and finish around noon. So once again we're up at seven, to drive our bleary-eyed and usually subdued passengers off for a morning among the stalls of food and flowers and antiques at Ile-sur-la-Sorgue. You may think it's an easy life we lead down here, but I can tell you that it places severe demands on your stamina as well as your liver.

And perhaps more than physical resilience, you need patience. When you have guests in the city, they haven't come solely to see you: they want to shop, to go to the theatre, to visit the galleries and see the sights. They leave the apartment in the morning, and you can usually tuck them into bed, footsore and happy, not much later than midnight. In the country there is less organised entertainment and fewer distractions, so the burden of amusement falls on the hosts. In our case, it doesn't stop at amusement, and we find ourselves running all kinds of strange and sometimes very personal errands when our guests' knowledge of French is limited to reading menus.

In the past year, we have been pressed into service to haggle with antique dealers, to dispute garage bills, to make a deposition to the police about a stolen handbag, to return to cancel the deposition when the handbag was discovered under the front seat of the car, to query the currency rates at the bank and to make innumerable changes of airline reservations. On our guests' behalf, we have become regular visitors to the local pharmacy, and we now have a small pharmacy of our own, filled with half-used remedies for diarrhoea and sunstroke, wasp stings, blisters, hay fever and ailments of an intimate feminine nature.

It's getting better. We have learned to say no to dimly remembered acquaintances who have a sudden desire to see us again, preferably for three weeks in July. The unlovely guests are not asked back a second time, and the people who stay with us now are people with whom we know we can live. And the pleasures of having them more than outweigh the effort and money involved.

It's good to see how they change in the course of a few days – from being tense and tired and pale to being tanned and relaxed. We like it when they seem to love Provence as much as we do, when they learn to play *boules* and take their first bicycle ride in years, when they stop looking at their watches and slow down to our pace. They are a hobby and a lot of fun and a reminder of our good luck at being able to live here, and we would miss them if they didn't come. They're a habit.

16

THE
SHIRT
DE LUXE

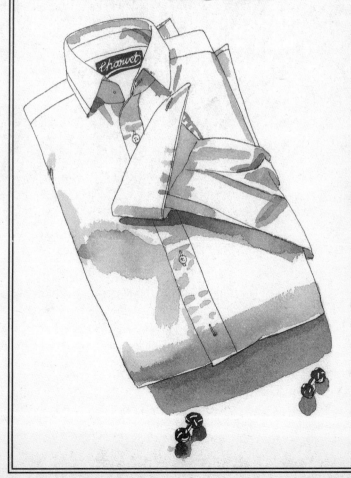

In the wardrobe of the Great Gatsby there were many shirts. 'Piled like bricks in stacks a dozen high ... shirts of sheer linen and thick silk and fine flannel ... shirts with stripes and scrolls and plaids in coral and apple-green and lavender and faint orange, with monograms of Indian blue.'

Gatsby was obviously an addict, and while one may have a few reservations about his weakness for coral and faint orange and scrolls – particularly the scrolls – there is no denying that a wardrobe stacked with shirts is a comforting sight. A man can never have too many. I certainly can't. And so it was with a light step and a trembling wallet that I went to pay a call on Charvet, the most famous shirt-maker in Paris, to discover for myself how it has managed to survive wars, recessions and the vagaries of fashion for 151 years.

Don't expect to find a mere shop. The house of Charvet, at 28 Place Vendôme, occupies several floors of some of the most distinguished real estate in Paris. The ceilings are lofty, and no effort has been made to cram the space with merchandise. There is plenty of room to twirl your silver-topped cane as you stroll through the displays of shirts and ties that are scattered like islands around the ground floor.

A man in the corner gave a final tweak to an arrangement of ties and came over to see if he could be of help. I noticed his shirt. He noticed mine. (It's a funny thing about makers of bespoke clothing. They can't help making a quick assessment of what you're wearing. It's instinctive. I hoped my tie was straight.) He smiled, and inclined his head when I said I wanted some shirts. He escorted me to a tiny elevator, and we went up together. He introduced himself as Joseph and made a note of my name on a pad.

We stepped out of the elevator and into a collection of shirts that would have made young Gatsby giddy with indecision. Joseph gestured at them with a sweep of his arm. What did I have in mind? These were ready-made shirts – of impeccable quality, *naturellement*. Or perhaps ... he paused, and right on cue I said I would prefer something made to measure.

Ah. In that case, said Joseph, I could choose between two possibilities. The first was full measure, when the entire shirt is constructed to your personal pattern. But there is a drawback: You need to return in ten days for an *essayage*, or fitting, and this is not always convenient for Charvet's clients. Much as I loved the idea of killing time in Paris for ten days, I had to leave the following morning. Joseph was unperturbed. There was no problem. I could have, instead, the second possibility, which, as he explained it to me, seemed the ideal solution for anyone who wants the advantages of bespoke shirts minus the ten-day delay. This system is called half-measure, and it works like this.

You try on a number of shirts until you find a body size that fits – across the shoulders, through the chest and waist, and with the correct length. The body of your shirts will be cut to that existing pattern. The rest will be made to measure, exactly to your requirements, and the shirts will be sent to you in three weeks. An inspired compromise.

I was shown into a changing room and given half a dozen shirts to try on. When we had arrived at a body size that felt comfortable and satisfied the experienced eye of Joseph, he telephoned for the *tailleur*, or head cutter – a dapper, exquisitely shirted gentleman with a tape measure draped around his neck.

The tape was transferred to my neck. Then he measured the distances between shoulders and elbows, and elbows and wrists, and finally the circumferences of the wrists themselves, allowing a little extra for the left cuff so that it would accommodate my watch. Joseph noted all the measurements on his pad.

Another escorted trip by elevator down to the fabric room, and here Gatsby would have expired from pleasure. There were silks and linens and poplins and Oxford cloths in plain shades, in tiny checks, in plaids and in every possible kind of stripe, from the barely visible to the barely bearable – bolts and bolts of fabrics, piled to head height and taking up an area as big as a millionaire's billiard room. I have never seen so much raw shirting in my life, and I asked the *tailleur* how many different fabrics there were. Thousands, he said. Nobody has ever counted. It would take a week.

It could have taken me almost as long to make a choice if I hadn't decided beforehand on a short list of colours and materials that restricted the possibilities to dozens rather than thousands. Even so, I was encouraged to spend a certain amount of time walking from one opulent pile to the next. Some shirt-makers will sit you down and bring you books of swatches, which I have never thought of as the best way to choose a shirt. A scrap of fabric four inches square is not enough to judge how the finished article will look. But with the bolts at Charvet – and a little patient assistance from Joseph – you can see how a fabric hangs and how you like the colour when you see an expanse the size of a shirtfront.

After an hour or so, I decided on some Sea Island cotton, which has the handle of silk without any of the laundering problems. Joseph approved, and took my bolts and me into a small, separate room where we could ruminate on the selection of collars and cuffs. Displayed on the wall like disembodied necks and wrists were tab collars, spread collars, collars with long or short points, with or without stiffening, barrel cuffs, French cuffs, fold-back button cuffs – once again, a variety of choices that could lead you very easily into an extended trance of pleasant dithering.

We chose, but Joseph was not quite finished with me. Would I like gauntlet buttons on the sleeves above the cuffs? These keep the opening between wrist and arm from gaping, and give a neat, flat finish. I said yes to the buttons.

And how did I feel about monograms? I said that I disliked them intensely, above all when they were displayed on a cuff, or when they were whimsically embroidered in those Japanese hieroglyphics that translate into 'keep your hand off my left breast'. Joseph nodded. He had once raised the question of monograms with an American client, and the answer was a growl: 'I know who I am.' No monograms.

We had one small piece of unfinished business to attend to, and that was what the French sometimes describe with pitiless accuracy as '*la douloureuse*' – the painful moment of settling up. Naturally, this required another escorted trip in the elevator. While we were waiting, I noticed a framed certificate on the wall. It was dated 1869, and it came from the Prince of Wales, who was graciously pleased to confirm that Monsieur Charvet was his official shirt-maker in Paris. (The prince evidently had a shirt-maker in each of the cities he visited regularly, perhaps to compensate for the slowness of nineteenth-century laundries.)

The payment of bills at Charvet is dealt with by a gentleman seated at a desk while a young lady at a table behind him folds shirts and scarves and ties into billows of tissue paper before laying them to rest in Charvet boxes. You can pay in cash, or with a cheque drawn on a French bank, or by credit card, but however you pay, you will need to exercise self-control to avoid a sharp intake of breath.

I have my bill in front of me. Gasp now so that you can preserve your sangfroid later. Each shirt cost 1,900 francs, or approximately £200. Admittedly, the Sea Island cotton that I chose is more expensive than poplin, and a ready-made shirt is a trifling £100. But it would be a shame to go to Charvet and not get the treatment – the leisurely tour of the fabric room, the pondering over collars and cuffs, the cosy elevator rides and the undivided attention of Joseph for most of the afternoon. That, for me, is a large and enjoyable part of buying made-to-measure clothes.

And I never have to go shopping again; not for shirts, anyway. I have Charvet's telephone number. Charvet has my pattern and measurements. If I want, I can sit here in Provence and spend thousands of dollars in the course of one short and reckless phone call, and three weeks later the mailman will stagger up the drive with an armful of Charvet boxes. On the other hand, going up to Paris is no hardship, and that fabric room deserves a second investigation.

Joseph wished me a pleasant evening and showed me out. The sun was going down behind the Place Vendôme, and I realised that Charvet possesses a unique advantage over other shirt-makers, one that has nothing to do with shirts. It is two minutes from the Hemingway bar at the Ritz.

17

NEW YEAR'S RESOLUTIONS

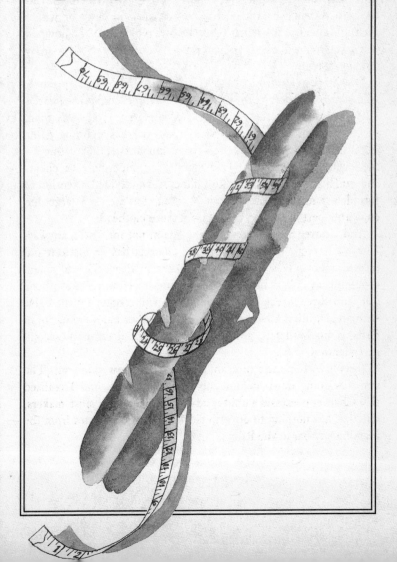

I t is 11.30 on New Year's Eve, and you're feeling wonderful. The vintage Krug is fizzing through your veins, beautiful strangers are lining up to kiss you at the stroke of midnight, and the New Year, as full of promise as a rich and indulgent uncle, lies ahead. A fine old time is being had by all. And then someone – there is always someone, and he or she is always drinking Perrier with a twist – comes up to you and asks:

'What are your New Year's resolutions?'

Oh, God. Who is this voice of doom, this hideous reminder of real life and restraint, just when the party is getting nicely out of hand? Well, if you don't recognise the voice tonight you certainly will tomorrow morning, because it is none other than your conscience, disguised in human form and waiting for you to renounce at least one of your reprehensible but highly enjoyable habits.

I don't know how it all began, or when that awful dose of self-denial was added to our otherwise carefree genes, but every New Year's Eve, all over the world, enough resolutions are made to render life on earth as much fun as a series of undertakers' conventions. Fortunately, as we shall see later, sanity eventually returns. But not before our resolutions have cost us dearly.

The second mistake (the first being to consider any resolutions at all) that most of us make is to broadcast our intentions. We can't keep our ghastly plans for self-improvement to ourselves. We have to tell everybody within conversation range what we have decided to do, and New Year's Eve being New Year's Eve, we are frequently drunk when we tell them. Not a good start, although the thought behind it is, in its own twisted way, commendable: we know that the flesh is weak, and so for moral support and as an aid to rubbery willpower, we commit ourselves publicly. Failure to deliver will result in the scorn and disapproval of our friends. Failure is out of the question. Failure is for wimps.

To make matters worse, it is not enough to make small, unobtrusive resolutions. Giving up trashy books, late-night television, banana fudge sundaes or yelling at cabdrivers may require a measure of self-discipline, but these sacrifices are all too private;

nobody else will know. And since one of the traditional horrors of resolutions is that they should have a visible effect, we once again fall into the trap (we are still in our fuddled New Year's Eve euphoria, remember) of making a Major Resolution.

This is not to be confused with business. Announcements about your next dazzling career move don't count, unless they involve a painful change in your circumstances, such as giving up Wall Street to become a monk. Otherwise, trying to pass off your ambitions as resolutions won't wash. So what are we left with?

In nine cases out of ten, the Major Resolution has something to do with physical appearance or health. (The mind takes a back seat on these occasions because mental achievement is not sufficiently visible.) In many of these cases, obeying the natural law that says every vacuum must be filled, the resolution requires two steps: give up a pleasant but unhealthy habit, and replace it with a healthy alternative. If this were as simple as cutting out ice-cream and taking up jogging, the financial side effects would be minimal. But it never is that simple.

Let's say you've really gone to town on New Year's Eve. You'll give up smoking and drinking, and you'll lose ten pounds by the time you hit the beach in the summer. You see the new, improved you in your mind's eye – a muscular, unpolluted Adonis, the envy of the wheezing, overweight wrecks around you.

The first day of January is no problem, since you have the mother and father of a hangover and all you can think of is to find the top of your head. As the month wears on, however, your resolutions begin to bite back. The bottle beckons, the very idea of a smoke is enough to make you giddy, and a large can of *foie gras* seems to follow you round the apartment. Stern measures are required if temptation is to be overcome.

And so you give temptation away to unbelieving but grateful friends: the case of 1955 port, the precious half-dozen bottles of ancient cognac, the humidor filled with the best that Alfred Dunhill can supply, the *foie gras* – get thee behind me, all of you.

This noble but costly gesture is soon followed by the realisation that you have abandoned one set of crutches and are in urgent need of another. Don't worry. The health and fitness industry is ready for you, flexing its pectorals and holding out the promise of cardiovascular bliss. All you need to do is choose your particular form of exercise and arrange a bank loan.

I suspect that one of the prime reasons for the spectacular increase in expenditures on fitness that we have seen over the past few years is the irresistible appearance of the equipment. The stuff looks terrific, all the way from aerodynamically designed sweat socks to the 135-station closet-sized gym. Training shoes look like sculptures. Tennis racquets could have come straight out of the Museum of Modern Art. The lowly dumbbell, once a dull lump of iron, is now chromed, striated and burnished until it resembles the crankshaft from the engine of a £100,000 Ferrari.

Very quickly you find out that none of it is cheap. But, you say to yourself, if you're going to take your resolutions seriously, you must be seriously equipped. It's not extravagance; it's self-improvement. In any case, buying the equipment can be fun. (A lot more fun, you soon discover, than using it.) And while you're at it, why not join other clean-living, iron-willed people in a gym or racquet club? And you do, in spite of the savagely expensive enrolment and membership fees.

Several hundred dollars lighter, you can now get down to work. It hurts. It is, as so often is the case with exercise, monotonous. After each session, the body aches, so presumably some beneficial changes are taking place, but there's no visible difference, no gasps of admiration from the women in the office, no dramatic or even faintly encouraging signals from the tape measure. The head tor-turer at the gym, a young man who appears to be made of polished marble instead of flesh and bones, insists that there's nothing to worry about. All it takes is time. How much time? Oh, three months, maybe six. Let's have another hundred sit-ups and then we can move on to the bench press.

Six months! They stretch before you, painful and alcohol-free, and you begin to wonder if the end is going to justify the means. If there is a hint of doubt in your mind, you've had it. I have no formal statistics on the resolution-failure rate, but personal experience and observation lead me to believe that it is at least as high as that of first novels or attempts on Mount Everest. As a general rule, trying to give up what you like to take up what you think you ought to do is a doomed endeavour.

Someone, I think it might have been Oscar Wilde, said: 'Moderation in all things – including moderation'. The wisdom of this is that it recognises man's natural instinct to lurch off the rails from time to time and go on a glorious bender; most resolutions refuse to take this into account. They are all or nothing, abnormally severe and, in their own way, a form of excess. That is why, some time around mid-February, millions of people with varying degrees of guilt or self-justification return to their old ways. The equipment is a daily reminder of non-achievement, so it is hidden or given away. And that, until next New Year's Eve, is that.

After many years of going along with this ridiculous nonsense, I have now kicked the resolution habit. I do have resolutions, but they are the same each year and so far I have managed to keep them. I offer them to you in the hope that they will do for you what they have done for me – that is, avoid unnecessary expense, banish guilt and make it possible to face the New Year with a clear and untroubled eye.

Resolution Number 1

I never, ever go out on New Year's Eve. Instead of the forced merriment and the consequent liver damage, I eat dinner at home with the most expensive bottle of wine I can lay my hands on. I take a glass of champagne to bed, and if I'm still awake when the New Year arrives I toast it. On New Year's Day, when the rest of the world is feeling terrible, I go out and have a very long lunch.

Resolution Number 2

I try on last year's trousers. In fact, I have a pair of trousers, now seven years old and part of a seldom-worn suit, that I keep as a benchmark. If they start to feel tight, I do something about it – nothing more excessive than a few days of reduced bread consumption (which, as I live in France, is usually at least a *baguette* a day) does the trick. The secret is to nip any expansion in the bud, when there's less to lose. It's easy, and it works. As my tailor can verify, my measurements have stayed the same since 1973.

Resolution Number 3

I never drink before breakfast.

These annual resolutions have now become habits, and for once in my life, they're not expensive. A prosperous New Year to you all.

18

THE HANDMADE HOTEL

I think it was Conrad Hilton who first had the idea that travel would be greatly improved if as much of it as possible were spent in familiar surroundings. Faraway places with strange-sounding names are all very well, provided there are scrambled eggs for breakfast, air-conditioning, brisk and efficient plumbing and people who speak English, even if they speak it with a curious accent. Let us, by all means, explore the native bazaars of Paris and penetrate the upper reaches of the Via Veneto. But what the weary traveller needs after being up to his neck in foreigners all day is a drink with plenty of ice, a straightforward dinner menu that doesn't require an interpreter, a decent bathroom and a king-sized bed. Just like home.

The Hilton theory was, as everyone knows, a worldwide success. And this was for one very simple reason: even if you didn't always know where you were, you always knew what to expect. There were no surprises. A few touches of local colour would creep in from time to time – mangoes instead of orange juice, waitresses in sarongs instead of skirts – but for the most part it didn't really matter whether you fell asleep in Tokyo or Mexico City. There was a certain standardisation about the board and lodging that provided comfort and reassurance and familiarity even in the heart of the most exotic locations.

If the idea had stopped there – as one among many travel options – it would have been fine. Unfortunately, it proved to be so popular that it was adopted by one hotel chain after another, with varying degrees of local camouflage designed to add personality to a multi-national formula. With loud protestations that they were preserving the special character of each hotel they gobbled up, the new owners standardised everything that could be standardised, from bathroom fittings to colour schemes, until the only sure way of knowing which city you were waking up in was to consult the phone directory as soon as you got out of bed.

All this might have disappeared as travellers became more so-phisticated and adventurous, had it not been for the emergence, about twenty years ago, of an affluent and influential patron in the hotel universe – a new breed of nomad who now pops up every-where on the urban world's surface. He is the ultimate guest, the big spender, the man who calls room service or Rio with no thought for the cost, the single most important and profitable customer a hotel could wish for. He's the busy, successful and generously funded globe-trotting executive, and most hotels today are designed for him.

As we live in an age when every aspect of human behaviour and preference is fed into the maw of a computer and analysed, there is no doubt that the new nomad's whims and fancies have been researched and studied down to the last detail. I myself have never seen the conclusions of this research on paper, but who needs a document? The evidence is clearly displayed in hotels all over the world. After doing some research of my own in America, Australia, Britain, France, Germany, Italy and Switzerland, I feel that I know exactly what our corporate hero requires from a hotel.

First, he needs a grandiose lobby, preferably an atrium with a young forest sprouting up around the furniture. This is not for aesthetic reasons, nor is it to make him feel that he has entered an oasis of sylvan calm after a day of savage cut and thrust. No. It is because he can use the lobby as a giant office. There is room to swing his attaché case. He can hold a conference beneath the ficus trees, order drinks, take calls, make presentations and generally treat the place like a temporary extension of Wall Street or Madison Avenue.

He needs several bars: one for business, with sufficiently good lighting for him to be able to read sales figures and contracts; one for dalliance (you never know who you might run into), with sufficiently bad lighting to ensure that there is no chance of being recognised by anyone more than ten feet away; and one in his room.

The room itself should be equipped with a variety of accessories and gadgets and forms that reduce the need for any personal contact with the hotel staff to a minimum. Instead of having to communicate by old-fashioned word of mouth, the executive can write memoranda to the hotel on the lists and pads provided: the laundry memo, breakfast memo, the bar-consumption memo and

so on. (One day, this will be superseded by an electronic command system which will enable the guest to punch into the breakfast mainframe or the dry-cleaning data bank, but the end result will be the same: modern, impersonal efficiency.)

This is presumably what the floating business population of the world likes to find on its travels. I don't. When I stay at a hotel, I like to feel that I'm a guest and not a transient unit in a convention centre. I like to enjoy those small and luxurious attentions that are impossible at home, and that only a diligent staff of two hundred can provide. To hell with streamlined and faceless modernity: give me the pleasure of being looked after by polite, well-trained, smiling people. In other words, give me a room at the Connaught.

It's easier said than done. The Connaught, the pride of London innkeeping, was built in 1897, when hotels resembled large houses instead of small office blocks. Consequently, the number of rooms is limited and most of them are occupied throughout the year by foreign royalty, the quieter members of American society, British landed gentry and the occasional distinguished actor. Even when rooms are available, a reservation is not necessarily automatic. It helps to know someone who has stayed at the hotel, almost like a reference, just to be sure that you are the kind of person who will be comfortable with the other guests, and they with you.

The main entrance, on Carlos Place, is small and polished, framed by flowers and presided over by a gentleman who is large and polished, from the silk of his top hat to the mirror finish of his shoes. He allowed my wife to carry her handbag; everything else in the taxi, from magazines to suitcases, was spirited away so that we could make an uncluttered arrival.

The lobby is tiny by contemporary standards, no bigger than your great-grandfather's study, and probably furnished in much the same way, with brass and glass and mahogany panelling, and carpets and chairs in those quiet colours that age gracefully until they achieve a kind of faded bloom. There is nothing to jar the eye, nothing too bright. Everything has a well-bred gleam – the brass, the glass, the mahogany and the teeth of the welcoming committee behind the front desk.

We were asked who we were, and from that moment on all the

hotel staff seemed to know us. How the information was passed along so quickly and so unobtrusively is a mystery, but from the chambermaid to the barman, everyone addressed us by name, a basic courtesy that I thought had vanished from hotels along with nocturnal shoe-cleaning and linen sheets.

A young man in a black tailcoat showed us up to our room and promised to do the best he could with the London weather. Luggage and afternoon tea arrived, and we were left to unpack, although I had the impression that if the journey up in the elevator had overtired us, someone would have been happy to unpack on our behalf.

We might have been in the bedroom of an English country house in the days when owners of country houses could afford to run them properly. There were fresh flowers on the table, and writing paper with the texture of new bank notes. Apart from the television set in the corner, the only concession to gadgetry was a tiny panel beside the bed with three buttons: one to summon the chambermaid, one for the waitress, one for the valet. Between these three, all things were possible. Should we find ourselves suffering from night starvation, a broken shoelace or a crumpled jacket, feel the sudden need for an extra pillow or an aspirin, want a pair of socks pressed or a hat steamed and brushed, a touch of the button would bring a member of our trio to the door within two minutes. It was how room service used to be, I imagine, before the invention of the telephone.

Almost as welcome as the nearby presence of helpful people was the absence of self-congratulatory literature – those overwritten puffs that most hotels cannot resist scattering throughout their rooms to promote their bars and restaurants and telex machines and conference facilities. Indeed, there was a sentence in the single sheet of guest information that was wonderfully discouraging to anyone with an attaché-case complex and a rabid work ethic. The sentence read: '*Business meetings in public rooms will not be welcomed.*' Work, like sex, should be conducted away from the view of other guests. The writer was a man after my own heart, and he was particularly firm on the matter of dress: '*No jeans.*' I warmed to him even more.

I suppose the truth of it is that I am a sartorial snob. Jeans, running shoes, ski jackets, tennis shirts, yachting sweaters, great-white-hunter outfits and Australian bush hats are all admirable garments in the right place and at the right time, but they look sloppy, incongruous and rather silly in the middle of an elegant hotel. Some people may think it's chic to look like an escapee from a logging camp, but not me. I like to be at least as well-dressed as the bellboy, and so I was quite happy to put on a tie for the first time in months before going down to the bar.

Serious bars are in short supply these days. Interior decorators and gardeners and musicians have been allowed to run riot and interfere with the central purpose of a bar's existence – that is, to provide solid, well-made drinks in congenial surroundings. It should be a simple matter; it rarely is. Either the lighting is so subdued that you can't find your drink without a flashlight; or the piano player has fingers of lead and a killer's compulsion to drown conversation; or the jungle of ferns and potted palms hides you from the waiter's view; or the drinks are given absurd names that are an embarrassment to honest alcohol. One way or another, it has become increasingly difficult to find a bar that isn't trying to be a social event or a stage set.

The original Harry's Bar in Venice is one of the few remaining havens for the man who wants to have a proper drink without unnecessary distractions, and the Connaught is another. The Connaught bar is, in fact, two interconnected rooms, furnished with small mahogany tables, leather club chairs and couches. Nobody stands at the bar except the barman, and so instead of having to look at a row of backs, as so often happens, you can watch an artist in action with bottles and glasses and cocktail shakers, quick and deft, doing his noble work with the relaxed precision that comes from twenty years of practice.

He is one of several people at the Connaught whom I would like to kidnap and bring home, but it would be a mistake to separate him from his other half, the bar waiter. This man is, without doubt, the best I have ever come across. He has a juggler's dexterity with loaded trays and brimming glasses, which is impressive enough, but what sets him apart from lesser waiters is the second pair of eyes he has in the back of his head. I also suspect him of telepathy.

He is constantly on patrol between the two rooms, ready to eliminate thirst wherever it may be, responsive to almost invisible signals. A raised finger or even the twitch of an eyebrow is enough to order a fresh round of drinks. There's no need to repeat the original order; he knows what you're drinking and seems to know how long it will take you to drink it, organising his patrol so that he comes within eyebrow range as the last mouthful is going down.

The drinks are the way drinks ought to be – good measures in sensible glasses, no frills. They are served with bespoke potato chips made that day in the hotel kitchens. The conversations going on around you are quiet and contented. There is no music. There are no business meetings. Calm prevails, life is good and the only major problem of the evening is to decide what to eat for dinner.

A man who looked as though he was on leave from the diplomatic corps arrived from the direction of the restaurant. He gave us menus and a leather-bound wine list the length of a short novel before gliding off to let us choose in peace from a selection of classic French and English dishes. He returned just as I was reading that dramatic chapter in the wine list in which the old clarets are breaking through the £300-a-bottle barrier. I went back to chapter one, and we ordered.

There are two dining rooms in the Connaught, and there is a certain amount of discussion, not entirely free from elitism, about which of the two is the centre of the universe. The hotel itself, very sensibly, keeps well out of this discussion, but there are those who will tell you that the Grill Room, particularly at lunch time, is where you are likely to see captains of industry and the more respectable politicians. In the larger restaurant, your companions will be run-of-the-mill duchesses and millionaires who are not burdened with affairs of state or concerns about the industrial health of the nation. Naturally, we chose to join these more frivolous customers in the restaurant.

Our departure from the bar was free of any suggestion that drinks might have to be signed for or paid for; at least, not there and then. Residents of the Connaught do not have to involve themselves with the detailed expenses of eating and drinking. When you have finished, you get up and leave. Nobody will come rushing after you waving the tab. You'll see it eventually, when you settle up at the end of your stay. Until then, bills are for other people, not you.

It takes very little time before you get used to this agreeable system, and we were told about a regular guest at the Connaught who decided one night to have dinner at Scott's, just down the street. He finished his meal, bid the headwaiter good night, and left to stroll up Mount Street before going to bed. He was shadowed at a discreet distance by a man with a bill. This was presented to the hotel, the necessary arrangements were made and the guest was not troubled.

There may be more fashionable places to eat in London than the Connaught, but it would be hard to imagine anywhere more comfortable. The tables are widely spaced, beautifully set and decorated with flowers, the large panelled room is softly lit – all the things you would expect to find in a formidably expensive restaurant. What we hadn't expected were such large helpings of charm. From the *maître d'hôtel* to the boy who wheels the roast beef up to the table for inspection, everybody behaved as though we were the couple they had been waiting all their lives to serve. They were more than professional. They were friendly, and many grand hotels are too busy being grand to be friendly.

And the food? It would be unkind to tell you how good the food was. There is a group of chefs – men like Anton Mossiman, Nico Ladenis and the Roux brothers – who are becoming as well-known in England as Bocuse and Troisgros are in France. The chef at the Connaught is not such a public figure, but he cooks like a saint, and our first two courses were faultless.

There was then a pause for the ceremony of the second table-cloth. My wife and I like to think that we don't qualify as the world's messiest eaters, and there were no more than a few crumbs of bread on the table as we sat back. These were removed. A fresh cloth of virginal whiteness was then unrolled across the table, glasses and bottles and plates being lifted and replaced with infinite delicacy, so that the final part of the meal could be served on a spotless and unwrinkled surface. It was a detail, not necessary but very pleasant, and typical of the touches that distinguish the Connaught from ordinary hotels.

We had cheese, dessert and coffee. Somebody, somewhere, had our bill in case we should want it, but we exercised the guest's privilege and left it unseen until the day of reckoning.

Upstairs in our room, linen mats had been placed on either side of the bed. They were embroidered with two messages. The first one, legible as you got into bed, read 'Good Night'; the second, legible from the opposite direction, read 'Good Morning'. I left my shoes outside the door, and we slept the sleep of the rich.

The next morning, my shoes looked as though they had been reconditioned overnight, and they shone considerably more brightly than the watery London sun. There's another man I'd kidnap if I had the chance. Shoe cleaning is a dying art in London, as a glance at most Londoners' feet will confirm, and doesn't exist at all where I live in France. If I could lure the Connaught shoe cleaner away, I'd treat him like a prince.

In the interests of research rather than hunger, we studied the breakfast menu. It was Victorian in its abundance, the kind of nourishment that Englishmen used to fortify themselves with before a hard morning chasing foxes or building an empire. There was porridge, there were kippers, there were kidneys, there were different breeds of sausage, there was coarse-cut bitter marmalade and a baker's range of breads. We had coffee and croissants and felt virtuous.

We dawdled as long as was decent over breakfast, postponing our return to the outside world. My wife wondered what it would be like to live here permanently, and decided that it would be no hardship. I wondered what lifetime residence would cost. A clue was waiting for me at the front desk, slipped inside a leather folder, the first and last bill I would see during our stay.

It has to be said that life at the Connaught is not for anyone on a modest budget, or indeed on any kind of budget at all. As the wise old millionaire once said: if you have to ask the price, you can't afford it. During our visit, we had confined ourselves to breakfast and one other meal each day. We had avoided magnums of champagne and the $500 bottles of claret, and we had not made beasts of ourselves with midnight snacks of caviare, Grand Marnier soufflés, the grouse that had just come into season or nightcaps of the 1948 vintage port. We had behaved with restraint and moderation.

Even so, the bottom line after three days was hovering around £1,500, excluding tips, and it may require a little mental adjustment to think of £350 a day as representing wonderful value for your money. As far as I'm concerned, however, that's exactly what it is.

Setting aside the excellence of the cooking and the physical comfort of the hotel, the Connaught's great attraction, and the asset that separates it from other expensive hotels, is the atmosphere created by the people who work there. They were, without exception, well-mannered and charming and supremely good at their jobs. To find people like this, to train them and to keep them, costs far more than any number of superficially impressive luxuries. All the marble lobbies in the world can't compete with friendly human beings who are anxious to please you. That's what you pay for, and it's worth every cent. It used to be called service. Now, because it has become so rare, it's called old-fashioned service. God bless it.

THE
MALT

It's very strange. We live in an age when man's interest in his body verges on obsession: every visible moving part is subject to daily scrutiny, internal functions are monitored at least once a year by people in white coats, youth is prolonged, wrinkles kept at bay, stomachs sucked in, vitamins gobbled up. Yet, in the midst of this feverish physical surveillance, one small but vital part of the human anatomy is suffering from consistent, deliberate neglect. The palate has become a second-class citizen, and the taste buds are an endangered species, threatened with extinction through boredom.

What has happened, presumably in the interests of more consistent nourishment, is that individual tastes and local flavours have taken a terrible beating at the hands of the mass-producers. A Third Avenue hamburger tastes exactly like a Champs Elysées hamburger. Chicken, once a bird, has been turned into a commodity along with pork and beef and lamb. And as for vegetables – when was the last time you ate a tomato, a potato or a salad that you didn't have to smother with sauce or dressing before there was any hint of flavour?

Bread like plastic, apples like wet socks, cheese with the delicate complexity of a bar of cheap soap, onions with no bite, spinach that would make Popeye choke. It all looks genuine, because everything from the lamb chop to the string bean is bred for appearance, but its resemblance to real food stops the moment you start to chew. It's enough to drive a man to drink.

Alas, even booze hasn't escaped the insidious tinkering that produces uniformity and blandness. Beers are lighter, spirits are paler and drier, wine is being contaminated with soda water, and sales of taste-free vodka are booming. Ice is used with such reckless abandon that drinks are numbed rather than chilled, and the serious drinker now risks frostbite of the tongue more than cirrhosis of the liver.

But all is not lost. Up in Scotland, there are men engaged in heroes' work. They are not concerned with providing refreshment for the millions, but a taste of heaven for the few. Slowly, carefully and in small quantities, they are distilling single-malt whiskies.

Basic scotch whisky, the kind you would be served in a bar if you didn't specify a brand, is a blend of as many as thirty different whiskies – malts and the less distinctive grain whiskies. They are blended together for two main reasons. The first is to achieve a smooth and widely acceptable taste that is less idiosyncratic than unblended whiskies. The second benefit of blending is that it guarantees consistency. A good blended scotch, such as a Bell's, a White Horse or a Dewar's, will never give you any unpleasant surprises. This is ensured by a master blender, who keeps a sufficient supply of malts and grains to maintain the balance that gives the brand its particular taste.

The next step up in the scotch hierarchy is also a blend, but one in which only malts are used. These blends – 'vatted malts' – reflect the characteristics found in perhaps half a dozen single malts. Often ten or twelve years old (the age on the label is the age of the youngest whisky in the blend), they can be legitimately described as 'pure malts'. More pungent and more expensive than regular blended scotch, they offer the student of whisky a chance to acquire a general taste for malt before moving onward and upward into connoisseur's territory: the single, unblended dram.

It is here that the taste buds can be given some thorough exercise, because there are more than a hundred distilleries in Scotland that produce single malts, not one of which tastes exactly like another. With a magnificent disregard for mass marketing, the single-malt men are content to make their own highly individual whiskies – smoky, peaty and as distinct from one another as are wines from different vineyards. Some single malts are matured in old sherry butts, some in old bourbon barrels, some in old port pipes; all of these add different elements to the flavour. There is no rigid universal formula, no standard recipe, no 'best' single malt. It's a question of personal tastes: the distiller's and yours.

But where among the Lagavulins and Lochnagars and Glen Mhors and Balvenies and Old Fettercairns do you start? You have more than a hundred confusing but delightful options, and there is a limit to the amount of research you can drink. My best advice, as a researcher of long standing, is to sample three very different single malts that I try to keep in the house despite the kind attentions of visiting friends. These three, which are not difficult to find, will give you an idea of the enormous range of flavours that can be found in what is technically the same drink.

The first is Glenfiddich: light, with just a touch of peat, and at least eight years old. It is generally considered to be an excellent malt for beginners, and it is the best-selling single malt in the world. One nip will tell you why a bottle of single malt is £20.

It is, however, outsold in Scotland by Glenmorangie (pronounced up there with the emphasis on the o, as in 'orangy'), which is aged for ten years in old bourbon barrels before being bottled and has what the malt men describe as a medium body. 'Morangie' is said to mean 'great tranquillity', which may or may not have something to do with the end result of an evening's enthusiastic consumption.

My third single malt is Laphroaig, pronounced La-*froyg*. It comes from the Scottish island of Islay, which would be my first choice of place to be shipwrecked, since it must have the highest concentration of whisky makers on earth: eight distilleries in the space of twenty-five miles. Laphroaig is a big whisky, bottled at either ten or fifteen years old, with a lot of peat in its flavour, together with another characteristic that, depending on the literary style of the taster, is said either to betray its proximity to the sea or, more bluntly, to have a whiff of seaweed about it. Don't let this put you off. The makers describe Laphroaig as the most richly flavoured of all Scottish whiskies, and they're not exaggerating.

So there you have three to start you off, with the pleasant thought of another hundred-odd to try. But to appreciate fully the subtleties of taste and colour, the sweetness of the malt and the dryness of the peat, you're going to have to revise your scotch-drinking habits.

Ice is forbidden. In Scotland, it is regarded as a more serious offence than wife-beating to anaesthetise a single malt with lumps of frozen tap water. Whisky should be drunk as you drink cognac, at room temperature. Water is allowed (indeed, some Scotsmen take their malt half-and-half, 'with plenty of water'), but it must be pure spring water that hasn't been laced with chlorine, fluoride or any of those other chemical blessings that health-conscious authorities insist we consume.

There is nothing complicated about drinking single malts. Unlike wines, they don't need to be opened beforehand to breathe, or to be decanted. They don't need glasses shaped like young balloons, swizzle sticks, slices of fruit, olives, sprinklings of salt or ritualistic paraphernalia of any kind. There are, as there always are, optional refinements concerning the size and form of your glass – a small cut-crystal tumbler sets off the whisky's colour beautifully, for instance – and when to drink a particular malt (light-bodies before dinner and something fuller afterwards), but there is nothing pretentious about single-malt whisky. It is a clean, honest drink that needs no ornamentation.

And it is reputed to be good for you. Nothing official, of course, but if you were ever to ask a Scottish doctor what he would prescribe for good digestion, a sound night's sleep and a long and healthy life, he would quite possibly suggest a daily tot of the malt. The same view is held by enlightened Englishmen, and it has been the subject of some learned discussion in the House of Lords.

Lord Boothby, arguing that the level of taxation on scotch should be reduced, put it like this: 'in the modern world, scotch whisky is the only thing that brings guaranteed and sustained comfort to mankind.' He was supported by one of his political opponents, Lord Shinwell (who had once tried to make scotch available under the British National Health Service). Shinwell went on to propose that members of the House of Lords should be allowed to claim scotch as an expense, 'since there is general consumption of this liquid by noble lords, and since many of them cannot do without it because it is in the nature of a medicine.'

Lord Shinwell was ninety-nine at the time.

THE
WRITING
HABIT

Next to the defeated politician, the writer is the most vocal and inventive griper on earth. He sees hardship and unfairness wherever he looks. His agent doesn't love him (enough). The blank sheet of paper is an enemy. The publisher is a cheapskate. The critic is a philistine. The public doesn't understand him. His wife doesn't understand him. The bartender doesn't understand him.

These are only some of the common complaints of working writers, but I have yet to hear any of them bring up the most fundamental gripe of all: the lifelong, horrifying expense involved in getting out the words.

This may come as a surprise to many of you who assume that a writer's equipment is limited to paper and pencils and a bottle of whisky, and maybe one tweed sports coat for interviews. It goes far beyond that.

The problem from which all other problems spring is that writing takes up the time that could otherwise be spent earning a living. The most humble toiler on Wall Street makes more in a month than ninety per cent of writers make in a year. A beggar on the street, seeing a writer shuffling toward him, will dig deep into his rags to see if he can spare a dime. The loan officer in the bank will hide under his desk to avoid saying no yet again to the wild-eyed and desperate figure looking for something to tide him over until he finishes the great novel. He knows that the man of letters is not a good credit risk. 'Writers' and 'money', like 'military intelligence', are not words that fit together with any conviction.

From time to time, of course, mistakes happen. Money originally sent off on some adult and worthwhile mission gets diverted somewhere along the way and finds itself in a writer's pocket. Its stay there is short; not, as any writer will tell you, because of foolish extravagance, but because of the demands of the profession.

The first of these is the need for peace, which is not easy to find these days. City living disturbs the concentration. That traditional haunt of the urban writer, the garret, has become insupportable; the landlord is forever hammering on the door for his $2,000 a month, and in the brief moments between his visits the cockroaches make a terrible noise on the bare boards, the dripping tap bores into the brain and the force-eight gale howling through the brown paper stuck over the broken window rattles the back teeth. Emigration to the country is the only solution. Look what it did for Thoreau.

But it can't be an old tar-paper shack miles from anywhere and anyone. That is too much peace. In fact, that's enough peace to send a man gibbering into the woods looking for a tree to talk to after a day spent on his own. Peace is all very well as long as there's a place to go when work is done, a place where a sympathetic ear can be found to complain to. And what better ear, who more sympathetic, than another writer? He knows how tough it is. He understands.

That is how writers' colonies come into being. And inevitably, as soon as they are established, they also attract agents, editors, publishers and owners of funky restaurants, as well as real-estate operators on the make. Peace and the simple country life gradually disappear. The local bar sprouts ferns and starts serving complicated drinks, and the whole place goes to hell. Time to move again.

But we can't allow these domestic upheavals to interfere with the act of creation; God knows, there are enough interferences as it is.

Let's take, for example, the question of research. To the outsider, this probably suggests a few hours in the library or half a dozen phone calls, and maybe that's all it used to be. Today, however, writers are expected – more than that, *required* – to produce work that is totally authentic in all its details. Imagination and a couple of blobs of local colour aren't enough; the reader has to know that the writer has been there and done it. Direct personal experience is the thing, and don't try to fob off that sharp young editor with anything less. You're going to write a novel about love and death along the Bolivian border? Wonderful? Off you go. See you in six months, and don't forget your cholera shots and medical insurance.

The writer in the throes of research can often be seen in some of the world's most uncomfortable and dangerous corners. (For some reason, presumably expense, very little research is conducted at the Ritz or in Palm Springs.) In Beirut, in Nicaragua, in the stews of Hong Kong and the oven of the Australian outback, you will find him soaking up the atmosphere, crouched intently over his notebook. But if you should look over his shoulder expecting to see the jewel-like phrase or the telling observation, you might be disappointed. The poor wretch is more likely to be doing his sums to see if his advance will stretch to a plateful of beans as well as a beer.

After a few months of this, and a brief but costly check-up in the hospital for exotic diseases, he is technically ready to start work. The ream of blank paper awaits. The pencils are sharp. A saga of epic proportions, the stuff of which Pulitzer Prizes are made, swirls around in his head.

But can he get the damn thing out of his head and on to the paper? He paces up and down. He stares out of the window (writers watch a lot of weather) and monitors the progress of a fly on the wall. Eventually, he recognises the problem as a severe case of writer's block. (Or, according to Arnold Glasgow, writer's cramp: 'an affliction that attacks some novelists between the ears'.) The words aren't ready to come out yet. A catalyst is needed, something to start the flow, and you can be sure that whatever the catalyst is, the writer isn't going to find it in the room where he works.

Cures for writer's block are many and various and usually involve getting into debt or into trouble. Women and drink are the two old favourites, but most writers, ingenious and creative fellows that they are, resist the straightforward solution of finding local women and local drink. They want a change of scene as well, preferably a few days of high-speed roistering in New York or Paris, draining life's cup to the dregs until the credit cards are cancelled. It is what Hemingway described as 'the irresponsibility that comes in after the terrible responsibility of writing'. Except that, in this case, the writing hasn't actually been done. But it will be, it will be.

And to help it along, now that the research has been done and the block has (we hope) been unblocked, it is time to call in modern technology so that the torrent of words can flow as fast as thought.

Those primitive pencils must go, to be replaced by the latest in desk-top computers, complete with the author's software package. It is even worth ambushing the loan officer at the bank for this; great steps forward in efficient productivity can be achieved here, and all for a miserable few thousand dollars.

At last! The words are beginning to come out, and none too soon either, because the spectre of deadline has become a constant companion, and those calls from the editor that used to be so friendly now have a distinct air of do or die about them. There is a thinly veiled threat that if the manuscript isn't delivered, the advance (by now long gone) will have to be returned.

This sets off a chain of events and emotions familiar to all writers. It starts with panic, as realisation dawns that time and excuses have both run out. Panic is followed by exhilaration, as the pages pile up and look increasingly promising – a bestseller at least, and possibly a movie too. Exhilaration is followed by relief, as the manuscript is delivered. Relief is followed by anticlimax when nothing much happens – and won't, for at least six months. And anticlimax is followed by massive doses of doubt and consolation.

The period in between finishing a manuscript and seeing a book is bleak. Nobody calls any more. It's too early for galleys. It's too early for reviews. It's too late to change anything. The work has vanished, and post-natal depression can easily set in unless the writer's reward system is activated to help him through the limbo months.

It may be a further plunge into the flesh-pots, a trip (this time without the notebook), a new hobby, an old flame, a second honeymoon. Whatever it is will undoubtedly involve another visit to the money-lenders, because no consolation worth having is cheap. But at least there is the hope of becoming a rich literary lion before too much longer.

Occasionally, just often enough to encourage optimism, this does happen, and we see the best-selling author toying with a six-inch Havana while he waits for the Brink's truck to come up the driveway with his royalties. But the odds are long. Most writers aren't so lucky. For them there is nothing for it but to try again.

Or to get a job, pay the bills, live a regular, orderly life and generally behave like a responsible member of society.

I don't know how other writers feel, but I'd rather live precariously in my own office than comfortably in someone else's. My powers of concentration in meetings have atrophied. Wearing a tie gives me a rash. Corporate routine makes me claustrophobic, and I have a deep horror of attaché cases, with all that they imply. The lure of the solitary endeavour, at whatever cost, is irresistible. Is it a habit or an affliction? I'm not sure. But I do know that a writer's life is the life for me. Please send the cheque by registered mail.

FEEDING
THE HAND
THAT BITES
YOU

Almost every day, in what we like to call civilised urban society, we are being mugged. It is only minor mugging, not usually physically violent, and it's perfectly legal. But it is mugging nevertheless. An empty, demanding hand is thrust at us, and we press money into it.

Of all the pleasant old customs that progress and affluence have twisted out of recognition, one of the most savagely twisted is the business of tipping. What used to be an occasional bonus for special effort and attention has become a nagging, continual obligation, a form of servile blackmail that is practised in varying degrees from the diner to the four-star restaurant, with countless stops along the way.

The origin of the word is interesting and revealing. According to the *Oxford English Dictionary*, 'tip' probably took on its present meaning some time in the seventeenth century, as part of what the dictionary describes with admirable accuracy as 'rogues' cant'. Somehow or other – maybe the passage of a century or two helped – the word has become respectable and the act of tipping unavoidable.

Today, the tip vultures are everywhere. In France, for example, a man diving into a public toilet in need of relief is likely to find a large, moustached woman glowering at him as he enters. In front of her is a saucer, suggestively sprinkled with coins. If he should fail to add to the collection, there will be muttered curses and possibly a farewell flick from a wet mop. In France, you are expected to pay for your *pipi*.

I have often wondered why it is that most of us are prepared to add a surcharge to what we have already paid for food or drink or services. What causes our endless generosity towards people who are often surly and careless? It can't be the original reason for tipping, which was to reward service above and beyond the call of duty. Can it be that we want to be liked by the tipping mafia, that we're happy to pay good money for the two-second twitch that passes for a smile? Or are we just benevolent souls who delight in helping the less fortunate by slipping them a little of the milk of human kindness, in folding form?

No, definitely not. Kindness has nothing to do with it. We tip because we feel, for one reason or another, that we have to – that if we don't, embarrassment or worse will be inflicted upon us, and that we'll be made to pay for not paying. Many and various are the pressures and unspoken threats involved, as this review of tipping and its motivations shows.

Tipping for insurance

The man in charge of the parking lot runs a speculative eye over your new car. 'Nice machine,' he says. 'Don't worry. We'll take care of it.'

Translation: Do you want to see your hubcaps again? Do you want to find your paint job scratched, your fender mashed and your tape-deck stolen?

Of course he'll take care of your car – providing you make it clear in advance that you'll take care of him when you come to pick it up. But that is amateur stuff compared to the mass extortion that takes place every Christmas in your comfortable and well-run apartment building. The doorman, the super who lives in the boiler room, the garbage-collection serviceman, the maintenance man – they're all in on the act, beaming with goodwill and the expectation of a well-filled envelope. Tip them if you know what's good for you; otherwise, be prepared for a series of domestic disasters in the year ahead.

Tipping for comfort

When you finally persuade the girl of your dreams to have dinner with you, don't ever think it's enough just to make a reservation at an expensive restaurant. Even expensive restaurants have cheap tables, carefully placed by the doors that lead into the kitchen so that you can enjoy the sound of smashing dishes and the curses of the chef as you eat. And don't expect prompt service. It is an established fact that the tables nearest the kitchen are the last to be served. To avoid them, have your money ready as the *maître d'* greets you. More on that later.

If you should go to a club after dinner, the same principle applies. Unless you want to spend the evening sitting next to a six-foot speaker vibrating with maximum decibels, tip someone – almost anyone – as you come in.

Tipping to avoid public ridicule

The undisputed champion in this situation is the Manhattan cab-driver. He will take you grudgingly where you want to go, at a dangerously high speed. It will be a most unpleasant journey, and you will be a nervous wreck at the end of it. But every cabdriver expects a tip as his divine right, and if it's below his expectations, watch out. As you turn to walk away, there will be a torrent of abuse: 'Hey! You! Here's your fucking dime! You need it more than I do.'

These exchanges, irritating as they may be, are at least quickly over. Much worse is the lingering humiliation that lies in store for anyone who tries to ignore the Miami Squeeze.

I'm sure it exists in other parts of the world, but I have never seen it carried out with more telling effect than in the cluster of pretentious restaurants within a few minutes' drive of Bal Harbor, where the squeeze is more popular than shuffleboard. It works like this: as you enter the restaurant, a man, for some reason dressed in evening clothes, swoops toward you, teeth and shirt-front gleaming. You have never seen him before in your life, but he insists on shaking your hand. This is the first test of your *savoir faire* and acceptability. If your handshake rustles with money, you pass the test. (Five pounds just about gets you through, £10 gets you a B+ and £20 is an A.)

If the shark in the tuxedo discovers that your hand contains nothing but fingers, he will look pointedly at his own empty hand. This is your second chance, the moment on which your dinner hinges. Grease the palm and all is well. Leave it ungreased and suffer the consequences.

You will be shown to a cramped table in between the two

swinging doors to the kitchen, tossed a menu and a wine list, and abandoned. You will be buffeted by the stream of waiters coming and going, but none of them will stop. You will try to catch the shark's eye, but it will always be looking at that fascinating patch of blank wall six inches above your head.

I have a friend, a hero in his own small way, who dealt with this treatment as it deserves to be dealt with. He got up from his seat and bodychecked one of the waiters to attract his attention. 'You know the area,' he said. 'Where can we get something to eat while we're waiting?'

Unless you enjoy confrontations of this kind, your meal will drag on, marked from time to time by reluctant visits from an offhand waiter, until you ask for the bill. That is the signal for the shark – the man who has pointedly ignored you all evening – to reappear, all teeth and charm, to ask you if you enjoyed your dinner.

Most of us would mutter something and escape as quickly as possible, but not my heroic friend. He looked straight through the *maître d'hôtel* as though he weren't there, got up and walked out of the restaurant. The *maître d'hôtel*, with the thick-skinned tenacity of an encyclopedia salesman, followed him out into the parking lot.

'Haven't you forgotten something?'

My friend turned round, took a £10 note from his pocket and held it under the *maître d'*s nose.

'This was for you,' he said.

The *maître d'* smiled. The squeeze had worked again.

And then my friend took out his lighter and set fire to the £10 note, waving it back and forth before dropping the charred fragment to the ground.

'Enjoy your evening,' he said.

There is no record of the *maître d'*s reply.

Satisfying gestures of this kind, of course, should be confined to those places and people whom you never want to see again. With your regular ports of call, you'd better resign yourself to the fact that your continued popularity and comfort will depend on whom you tip, when you tip and how much you tip. We'll leave aside those once-in-a-lifetime encounters that are truly worthy of reward – the tax man who believes you, the mechanic who fixes your car on time, the courteous sales clerk at Bloomingdale's – and concentrate on three major centres of the gratuities industry.

Bars

Don't waste your time trying to calculate how much to leave; the bartender will do it for you by soaking an appropriate part of your change in a puddle of vermouth. When you finish drinking, simply pick up the dry money and go. In more elegant establishments, add ten per cent to the bill. The management has already slipped in a substantial charge for ice cubes, so anything more would be excessive.

Hotels

I have found that tipping in advance improves the level of service and avoids the embarrassment of being ambushed in the lobby at the end of your stay. Scatter your largesse on arrival, when it can do you the most good. Don't forget the doorman: a couple of dollars on a dry day will make sure he produces a cab in a downpour. Unfortunately, advance tipping doesn't work for room service, and I have yet to work out how to reduce the waiting time for a club sandwich and a beer to less than forty-five minutes.

Restaurants

A sly and greedy practice has developed in some restaurants that will be stamped out only if enough of us stamp. In many cases, a $12\frac{1}{2}$ or 15 per cent service charge has already been quietly built into your tab, and if you're not careful you could be adding a tip to the tip. Have no part of it. Ask the waiter if service has been included. If it hasn't, tip him. And don't automatically hand over 15 per cent – on a three-figure tab, 10 per cent is quite enough, in my opinion.

Always tip the *sommelier*, who can steer you towards the hidden jewels on the wine list on your next visit. Never tip the salad waiter, a dreadful Californian invention that should not be allowed in any serious restaurant. And be kind to the cloakroom girl. You never know. She may send you out in someone else's vicuña overcoat.

22

THE PRIVATE JET

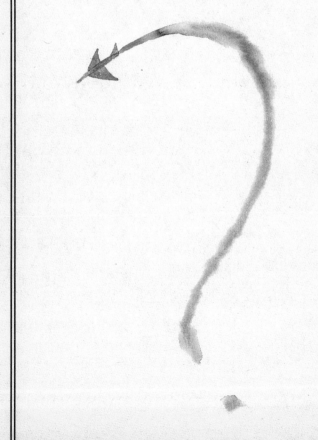

Once or twice a year, our friend Felix the tycoon comes to Provence for sunshine, French cooking and a brief escape from the cares of his office. I'm not quite sure what he does – a little high finance, the odd merger, an occasional dip into real estate – but it always involves several guarded phone calls as soon as he arrives at the house, and his attaché case is always bulging with the latest information on cocoa futures or corporate high jinks. But whatever the deal of the moment may be, it is put aside twice a day for the pleasures of the table. Felix loves his food.

It was spring when he last visited us, and over dinner he was discussing his favourite subject: the next meal. Where would we like to have lunch tomorrow? What he had in mind was fish, perhaps one of those garlic-charged *bouillabaisses* that can only be properly made by a French chef with fresh Mediterranean fish. And of course, he said, the only possible place to eat something like that is at a restaurant that overlooks the sea.

There is no shortage of food with a view in our part of Provence – restaurants that overlook mountains, rivers, fountains, village squares, vineyards, valleys – almost any view is locally available except a view of the sea. The nearest temple of *bouillabaisse* is in Marseilles, sixty miles away and a nightmare when it comes to parking. Even for a good gastronomic cause, that's a long haul. We asked Felix to think again.

He looked up from the assortment of cheeses that he had been deliberating over and beamed. Distance, he said, was not a problem. Nor was parking. He had brought his plane. It was at Avignon airport, a mere twenty-five minutes away, ready to take us wherever we wanted to go. The world was our oyster. Or lobster. Or even *bouillabaisse*.

By 9.30 the next morning we were at Avignon airport. Small and informal, it's the way airports used to be when flying was fun. There was no standing in line to check in, no officious ground staff to herd us into a departure lounge, no waiting, no fuss. The pilot and his co-pilot met us, and together we strolled out to the plane.

It was a business jet, cream on the outside and quiet pale grey in the cabin. There were seven seats covered in glove leather, personal stereos, coffee and drinks in the stamp-sized galley in the back. It was rather like the Concorde, but without that exasperating running commentary they insist on giving you, and with more leg-room. Felix told us it could cruise for four or five hours between refuelling stops, which meant that anywhere in Europe was within reach. As it happened, he had some business to do in Nice before lunch, so that Mediterranean city was our first stop.

We flew south until we reached the coast and then turned left, staying low enough to give us a continuous panoramic view of the Riviera. Felix consulted his restaurant notes as we passed over the towns and ports that shone in the morning sun. Let's see now. There's Le Chabichou in Saint-Tropez, Le Palme d'Or on the Croisette in Cannes, Belles Rives in Juan-les-Pins, La Bonne Auberge in Antibes – he made small humming noises of con-tentment at the thought of what the master chefs below us might be preparing. What a choice! What a choice!

The jet glided into Nice, and we had a pilot's-eye view of the landing. Before the engines were even cut off, a car was on its way across the tarmac to pick us up and take us to the terminal. A decision had been made about the restaurant. We were going to Cap d'Antibes, and, to avoid battling the traffic back to Nice afterwards, we would meet the plane at Mandelieu, the small airport just outside Cannes.

A young man in impenetrable sunglasses and a designer suit met us at the terminal and massaged us into a stretch Mercedes Benz. Felix was off to buy a bank or a yacht, or maybe both. He waved aside the details. What was really important, he said, was that we should do a little shopping for him before lunch, some provisions for his kitchen at home. Armed with a list and the Mercedes, we headed for the old flower market.

The Rue St.-François-de-Paule, which leads into the market, is notable for two well-established and delightful shops that could make a statue's mouth water. The first is Pâtisserie et Confiserie Auer, for chocolates and pastries and jams; the second is the tiny olive-oil kingdom of Alziari.

The girl who served us in Auer was impressed by the jam

requirements that Felix had scribbled down; *un vrai connoisseur de confiture*, she called him as she packed a huge assortment of jams made from clementines, bilberries, apricots, tiny bitter oranges, plums and melons. Did we have transport for this enormous carton? Indeed we did. As Felix had pointed out, you can buy in bulk when you have a plane to take the purchases home.

We went across the street and into Alziari. The shop is small and made smaller by the ceiling-high stainless-steel vats filled with first-pressing olive oil, described, with typical Gallic bravado, as 'extra virgin'. We were invited to taste a teaspoonful before committing ourselves. Virginal and delicious. We placed the order for several dozen litres, and while they were being drawn off from the vats and sealed in five-litre cans we worked our way down the rest of the list: three kilos of fat black olives; a dozen bottles of raspberry vinegar; jars of mild, almost sweet, anchovies in oil; pots of the olive paste called *tapenade*; packets of saffron; tubs of lavender-scented honey. By the time we were finished, there were two more enormous cartons, and the trunk of the Mercedes was beginning to resemble a comprehensively stocked gourmet store.

Felix joined us for a *pastis* in one of the bars alongside the flower market. He looked preoccupied, and I asked him if there had been a hiccup in his business dealings. Certainly not, he said. But on his way to the café, he had seen some exceptionally large and handsome *langoustines* and was now of two minds about what he should have for lunch. He communed with his appetite all the way to Cap d'Antibes.

Bacon, which one of the stomach bibles claims is the Rolls-Royce of seafood restaurants, rises like a perfectly cooked soufflé above the narrow coast road. The sea view is wall-to-wall, and the dining room is lighted by diffused sunshine. Felix rubbed his hands in anticipation as we went in, and his nostrils twitched at the scent of grilling fish, herbs and garlic. 'All great fish restaurants,' he said, 'smell like this.'

A middle-aged couple, she decorated with jewels and he with a major moustache, were bent in devotion over a steaming tureen. They both wore bibs, and as they watched the waiter transfer the contents of the tureen to deep dishes, they rubbed small rounds of toast with cloves of fresh garlic before spreading on a thick layer of rust-coloured sauce – the *rouille* that gives the fish stew a final pungent kick.

The main course was decided. To get into the spirit of the occasion, we started with mouthfuls of sea bass wrapped in a gauze of pasta and moistened with a truffle sauce. The white wine came from Cassis, a few kilometres away. We had travelled farther than anything on the menu.

Our tureen arrived, together with the trimmings and the bibs, and the waiter filleted the fish with just a spoon and a fork, deftly and quickly. He would have made a fortune as a surgeon. He murmured, '*Bon appétit*' and left us to it, and I wondered why it is that the best meals are often the messiest to eat. After twenty minutes with the garlic and the *rouille* and the rich, soupy juice, I felt that I needed a bath.

Lunch stretched into two hours, then nearly three, as lunches tend to do in France, and, a creature of bad habit, I began to worry about getting to the airport on time. Felix ordered more coffee and leaned back in his chair. 'What you have to remember,' he said, 'is that the plane doesn't go anywhere until we're ready to go. We decide the schedule. Have a calvados and stop thinking like a tourist.' I did both. It was wonderful.

We eventually got to the Mandelieu airport and loaded the gourmet store into the back of the plane. There was no word of reproach from the pilots. They'd been sunbathing. As we took off, I thought that I could very easily become used to this civilised and leisurely way of hopping round Europe, free of the time pressures and the cramped aggravation that have reduced airline travel to the same level of enjoyment as that of a subway ride at rush hour.

Was it, I asked Felix, completely beyond the resources of the normal wallet?

It all depends, he said. For instance, if one person were to take the plane from Avignon to Paris, the cost would be substantial – around 48,000 French francs, or £5,000, for fuel and landing fees. Mind you, he said, the plane lands in Paris only a few hundred yards from where the Concorde takes off, so if you were in a hurry to get to New York City, that would be the quickest way to go.

But there's another way of looking at it. Let's say your company has offices all over Europe, and let's say that four of you need to visit those offices in as short a time as possible. Amsterdam, Paris, Zurich, Milan and London could all be comfortably fitted into a work week. Plans could be changed and meetings could run over and it wouldn't matter. You would never miss your flight. It's not only convenient, it's also the most time-efficient method of shifting busy executives around. And it would cost, in total, only about double the first-class commercial airfare for one.

I said that it sounded dangerously close to being a bargain.

Exactly, said Felix. If you're doing business all over Europe, it makes perfect, comfortable sense.

I'm sure he's right. But I shall always think of it as a hell of a way to go to lunch.

23

MANHATTAN

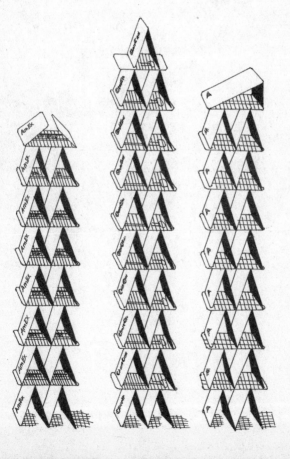

MANHATTAN was once kind to me when I needed a break, and I've had a soft spot for the place ever since. I had been trying to get a job in London as a copywriter. It was a hundred years ago, very early in the Sixties, and London advertising agencies were run by elegant and mostly rather unintelligent men who had been to Eton and Oxford, and who liked to surround themselves with young gentlemen from equally elitist backgrounds. I had not been to Eton or Oxford or indeed any university. Nor was I elegant. With such severe social handicaps, I was unable to persuade anyone to give me an interview for what used to be called a position – not even a position in the mailroom. And so, in the grand tradition, I decided to join the huddled masses yearning to be rich and travelled on the *Queen Mary* by subeconomy class (below the waterline) to the old pier at the end of West 52nd Street.

Manhattan was a revelation. Anything was possible, often by the end of the week. Hard work was rewarded generously and instantly. And to my great relief, nobody gave a damn about Eton or Oxford. I'm sure I was lucky, and I'm sure there were many who weren't so lucky. But I have marvellous memories of Manhattan. For me, it was a special town.

It still is, fortunately for different reasons than as a haven from unemployment. When I go there now, it's for a vacation, for the most complete change possible from my everyday life in the boondocks of Provence, for a dose of electricity and for fun.

You've probably never heard this from anyone else, but I *almost* enjoy going through Immigration. It's so quaint. The man in the uniform searches in his computer, eyes glazed with boredom, for traces of my criminal record and draws a blank. But he doesn't give up. Here comes his trick question.

'What is the purpose of your visit?'

I'm always tempted to bring a few moments of interest to his day, to try to deglaze his eyes and to give him the feeling that he is guarding America from the forces of evil. The purpose of my visit, Officer? Oh, just the usual – mainly racketeering and a little light pimping. Perhaps some narcotics trafficking if I get a spare moment, but you know how it is in Manhattan; there never seems to be time to fit everything in.

I wonder if he'd even blink. He'd probably scrawl 'business' on the forms and wish me a nice stay.

With the formalities out of the way, I can start to make serious inroads in my travel allowance by getting into town from the airport with the proper degree of self-indulgence. A cab is out of the question. So is the helicopter service: I tried it once and was deeply disappointed by the lack of civilised facilities. By the time I'd discovered that there was no bar, it was too late to get out.

Since then, I've used a limo, and to make sure that everything is as it should be, I call ahead to tell them not to forget the champagne. With traffic the way it is nowadays, a man could die of thirst in a four-mile traffic jam through Queens.

So here I am, feet up and bubbles in hand as the lights of Manhattan appear on the horizon. My credit cards tremble with anticipation, and I look forward to my first brush with the natives, who provide one of the best shows in town: Drama, low comedy, grotesque characters, pungent language – it's all there, and it's free.

There is a man, usually squatting on the sidewalk at the corner of Sixth Avenue and 42nd Street, who glares at every pretty woman who passes by and mutters at each of them 'Change your underwear, babe.' They pretend they haven't heard him, but you can tell that they have.

There are the early evening *mano a mano* contests, in which two executives dispute over a taxi. The dialogue is wonderfully predictable:

FIRST EXECUTIVE: 'That's my cab, you asshole!'
SECOND EXECUTIVE: 'Who are you calling an asshole, you asshole!'

Confrontation and abuse are everywhere, and I suspect that a lot of it is put on for hicks like me, just to let us know that we've stumbled into the big city.

And what an opulent, toy-filled, money-gobbling place it is, with everybody, it seems, hell-bent on conspicuous consumption. Messengers with £75 Reeboks, businessmen with handstitched crocodile attaché cases, middle-aged matrons staggering under the weight of their earrings, block-long limos on the ground, personal helicopters in the air, money being used up like oxygen – no matter how many times I go to Manhattan, I am always in shock for the first twenty-four hours at the speed with which a wad of bills turns into a pocketful of change. The solution, of course, is to avoid using money altogether, to switch to plastic and close your eyes when signing. Once I've made that simple adjustment, I can start to enjoy myself in suitably carefree style.

There is such a giddy diversity of money-blowing opportunities in Manhattan that it would take superhuman stamina and organisation to take advantage of them all in the space of a few days. I try, heaven knows I try, but I never manage to accomplish as much as I want to. There are, however, certain rituals that I observe on each visit. These are obligatory and take precedence over the bouts of wretched excess that lack of time usually prevents me from enjoying. Never mind. There's always the next visit. Meanwhile, I ease into extravagance with a trip to the barber.

Maybe I shouldn't call him a barber, because he is a haircutter whom other haircutters acknowledge to be one of the best in the world. His name is Roger Thompson, and his salon is downstairs at Barneys. He is often booked up for weeks in advance, and he has been known to turn away clients if their ideas about the right cut conflict with his. Put your head in his hands, and let him do what he wants. It will be the best haircut you've ever had, and it will cost you about £70.

My next stop, en route to lunch, is the Park Avenue shoe shop Susan Bennis Warren Edwards. Whether this is one person with a long name or two people working together without the benefit of punctuation I don't know, but somebody in the establishment has a fantastic eye for a well-formed shoe – simple, classic, immediately comfortable, breathtakingly expensive. Prices start somewhere north of £150 and accelerate rapidly if you should set foot in one of the more exotic leathers. A handsome felt bag is always included, as if you had bought emeralds.

Two minutes away is one of my favourite restaurants outside France. I was first taken to the Four Seasons at an impressionable age, twenty-five years ago, and I had never seen anything like it. I still haven't. The decor is stunning, with an attention to detail that is quite extraordinary. And then – another free show – there is the discreetly upholstered human furniture.

If fate were ever unkind enough to let a bomb drop on the Four Seasons at 1:30 in the afternoon, the publishing business would be left like a headless chicken. There they are, the top editors, the top agents, the seven-figure-advance authors, whispering in zeros about paperback rights and film options while they pick with disinterest at their spa lunches. Even worse, they're drinking water. Water, for God's sake, when the wine list is throbbing with promise and the sommelier is waiting to take you by the hand and lead you through the Burgundies. How can they resist? I certainly can't. Beside, I hate to see a lonely wine waiter.

A hundred or a hundred and fifty pounds lighter, I feel sufficiently refreshed to deal with the rest of the afternoon's business, which I try to divide between the equally appealing worlds of commerce and culture.

Compared to New Yorkers, I am not a true shopper. I don't have the stamina to work my way up and down Madison Avenue, rooting around among the cashmere socks and vicuña jackets and shot-silk suspenders, my arms growing longer with the weight of countless shopping bags, my overheated credit cards melting at the edges. I watch them, the true shoppers, their eyes gleaming with the lust to acquire, and I have to admire their tireless enthusiasm. I can only shop in short bursts, and I need professional help, someone who knows exactly what I want even if I'm not at all sure myself.

That's why, on practically every trip, I can't resist going to the West 40s, the nerve centre of electronic gadgetry and laser-fast salesmanship.

There are dozens of these stores, bursting with miniaturized marvels of high technology that are unheard of back home in provincial France – turbo-driven pencil sharpeners, underwater cameras, vest-pocket answering machines, digital pulse meters, eavesdropping equipment, featherweight video cameras, radios that are small enough to swallow. Do I need any of these extraordinary things?

I have to wait no more than five seconds for the answer, because that's all it takes for one of the salesmen to sprint the length of the shop and block the exit, talking deals and discounts and a year's supply of free batteries before I've said a word. These boys are dynamite. One of them, on his own, is somehow capable of surrounding you entirely. Leave it to him. He will tell you what you absolutely must have. A floating phone? A voice-activated alarm clock? A pen that writes in space? You got it. And how about a personal stress monitor with a biorhythm readout? Here. Take my card. Come back soon. Have a nice day.

When I eventually escape, it is to the relative calm of bookstores or the Museum of Modern Art. But even this is demanding, thirsty work, and by six o'clock I am drawn, as if by some primitive migratory instinct, to somewhere cool and dimly lighted where I can consider how to spend the next few hours. It is during these reflective moments that the possibilities for wretched excess come to mind.

One is to have dinner at the Palm restaurant on Second Avenue and to go fifteen rounds with one of those monsters in the pink-shell overcoats. The waiters there must be used to the customers' looks of disbelief when the carcass is served. 'What's the matter?' they say. 'Haven't you ever seen a lobster before?'

Or there is a ride down Fifth Avenue. I have heard about a limo that has a jacuzzi in the back, and the thought of careening through town stark naked and raising my champagne glass to startled pedestrians is enormously appealing.

I haven't done it yet, but I will. I'll report back.

CHER AMI

Cher Ami

Foie Gras
Confit de canard
Coquilles à la provençale
L'Escargots
Jambon d'Auvergne
—
Faisan normand
Caille feuilles de Vigne
Rognons de veau flambé
La Poule roti entier
—
Fraises des bois
Nougatine glacée
Ananas au Kirsch
Glace à l'abricots

The great Antoine died some years ago, in circumstances that I will come to later. But Chez L'Ami Louis, the restaurant that he owned and cooked in for more than fifty years, is still as he must have liked it: crowded and noisy, resolutely shabby, with a decorative sprinkling of pretty women ignoring their diets as they eat meals of nostalgic size.

This is rumoured to be the most expensive *bistrot* in Paris. I prefer to think of it as a bargain for anyone who is not ashamed of being hungry. People who toy with their food, or who profess a liking for large expanses of empty plate with tasteful dribbles of raspberry *coulis* in the centre – these poor scraggy souls will be horrified at the abundance. If you are one of them, read no further. You will only suffer vicarious indigestion.

Chez L'Ami Louis is number 32 in the narrow, nondescript rue du Vert-Bois, where the sounds of heavy breathing were once louder than the traffic. This used to be a neighbourhood for assignations, a *quartier* in which every other building was a hot sheets hotel. Ladies and gentlemen could rent rooms by the hour in the *maisons de passe* before tottering round the corner, still slightly flushed, to recover at Antoine's table.

Even in today's less carefree and naughty times, it is possible to imagine that the well-barbered man and his deeply *décolletée* companion whispering in the corner are taking an evening off from marriage, untwining their fingers and glancing up each time the door opens to see if it's anyone they know. Is it guilt, or are they just looking for famous faces? Politicians and statesmen, Roman Polanski, Faye Dunaway, members of the Peugeot family, Caroline of Monaco's ex-husband, the *beau monde*, the *demi-monde* – they have all been here, and no doubt they will all be back.

But why? It is difficult enough to sustain the success of a restaurant for five years before fashion kicks the chef in the teeth and moves on to newer, smarter tables. How is it that a small and ramshackle establishment in an undistinguished street has been able to flourish since the 1930s? Even more remarkable, it is Parisians rather than tourists who have kept the restaurant busy;

and Parisians, according to popular legend, are fickle and spoiled for choice. So why have they come, and why do they keep on coming?

Some of the best things in life are delightful accidents rather than deliberate inventions, and I have a feeling that Chez L'Ami Louis falls – or rather sits, knife and fork at the ready – into that category. There is a formula, if you can describe wonderful ingredients simply cooked and served in absurdly generous portions as a formula, but there is more to the place than that. It has a personality, a lusty air of appetite and unbuttoned enjoyment, and I suspect that this is the legacy of Antoine, whose ghost runs the restaurant.

You see Antoine's photograph at the far end of the room as you come in – a great, grey-whiskered badger of a man, who in his prime weighed well over 200 pounds. He looks out from his photograph at a view that has hardly changed in half a century. The black and white tiled floor has been worn down in patches to bare concrete. A venerable wood-burning stove squats at one side, its rickety tin flue slung precariously across the ceiling. The walls are the colour of roasted leather, black-brown and cracked. Straight-backed wooden chairs, narrow tables with salmon pink cloths, voluminous napkins, plain and serviceable cutlery. No artful lighting, no background music, no bar, no frills. A place to eat.

The manager for the past fourteen years (whose name, appropriately, is Louis), as solid as a steak in his white jacket and black trousers, shows you to your table. The waiters take customers' coats – cashmere, sable, mink, it makes no difference – roll them up and toss them with the practised two-handed flick of basketball players on to the head-high rack that runs the length of one wall. Gentlemen who wish to remove their jackets are permitted to do so, and are encouraged to tuck their napkins well up under the chin. The menu arrives.

It is a single sheet of white card, hand-lettered and brief: five entrées, ten main courses, five desserts. The choice varies with the seasons, and there are many clients who time their visits to coincide with the arrival of fresh asparagus, the baby lamb or the wild *cèpes*.

By early December, when I was there, winter had come to the menu; it was thick with the kind of food that clings to the ribs on a cold night.

The first course of any good meal is anticipation, those marvellous, indecisive minutes with a glass of wine in the hand and the imagination dithering over the possibilities. A *confit* of duck? Some scallops, throbbing with garlic? Roast pheasant? Quail cooked with grapes? From where I was sitting, I could see into the kitchen, a blur of white-clad figures and copper skillets. I could hear the sizzle of meat and smell potatoes turning crisp. A waiter came past balancing a flaming dish at shoulder height. Veal kidneys *flambé*. He was followed by Louis, nursing a dusty bottle. Our waiter came and hovered.

When in doubt, my Uncle William always used to say, have the *foie gras*. In fact, it is one of the classics of the house, supplied by the same family for two generations and said to have reduced many a gourmet to whimpers of delight. Yes, some *foie gras* to start with, and then a little roast chicken.

I thought the waiter's knife had slipped when he came back. There were four of us, and we had each ordered a different entrée. But there was enough *foie gras* for us all – dense pink slabs, finely veined with pale yellow goose fat and served with warm slices of *baguette* striped from the heat of the grill. The other plates were covered with equally immodest portions of scallops, of country ham, of *escargots*. A second warm mountain of bread in case we should run short.

It is either a shameful admission of greed or a tribute to the responsible attitude that I bring to research, but I tasted everything, and I can say that I've never eaten a better dinner. Unfortunately, the main course was still to come. I was beginning to see how Antoine used to maintain his fighting weight.

He had started his career, so I was told, as a *chef particulier*, a private cook in a wealthy household, and one can imagine the terrible void he left in the family stomach when he went public, and came to the rue du Vert-Bois. Only two things in life could distract him from cooking; he loved horse-racing and adored women. His favourite female clients were regularly smothered with garlic-scented embraces, and felt the touch of Antoine's oven-warm fingers on their cheeks. And the ladies adored him. One evening when a world-famous beauty was experiencing some technical difficulties with her garter belt in the ladies' room, it was not a woman who was asked to come to the rescue, but Antoine. He returned to the kitchen shaking his head in wonder, his hands forming voluptuous, quivering shapes in the air, muttering through his beard, 'What *magnificent* thighs'.

As it happened, my next course was an equally voluptuous chicken. When I ordered it, I had overlooked a crucial word on the menu, which was *entier*. The whole bird, shiny skinned, honey brown, moist with juices and resplendent of thigh, was carved with a dexterity that I always admire and can never achieve. (The victims of my carving, for some reason, have bones in unnatural places.) Half of this statuesque creature was put on my plate. The waiter promised to keep the other half warm for later, and delivered the *pommes frites* – a six-inch high pyramid of plump matchsticks that snapped softly between the teeth.

Miraculously, I finished part one of the chicken while my friends dealt with their more reasonably sized young partridges. To the polite surprise of the waiter, I was unable to come off the ropes for a second round with the chicken, but he didn't give up before threatening me with dessert. Wild strawberries? A *nougatine glacée*? A football-sized pineapple drenched in Kirsch?

We finally settled for coffee, and an after-dinner stroll to the kitchen, which I hope will be officially recognised one day as a national monument. It is manned by Bibi, Didi and Nini, who somehow turn out spectacular food in a small area almost completely devoid of modern equipment. Twenty or thirty battered copper pans hang over a blackened cast-iron range that was installed in 1920. The hotplates have worn through twice in seventy years, and have been replaced, and the heat is provided by wood – old, well-seasoned oak. And that's it. No microwaves, no gleaming computerised ovens, no expanses of stainless steel. The kitchen editor at *House & Garden* would have a fit.

But it works, so why change it? Anyway, change is out of the question. When Antoine was reaching the end of his career, he agreed to sell the restaurant on two conditions: the first was that it should be preserved in its original state; worn floors, rickety stove, cracked walls and all. As for the food, that too should continue to be as it always had been – the best ingredients, plenty of them, simply cooked. The second condition was that his wife should be taken care of when he died.

The legend of Antoine's death begins with his profound dislike of medical fuss and doctors. When he became ill, his friends pleaded with him to go to the best doctor in Paris. He refused. In that case, said his friends, we will arrange for the doctor to come to the restaurant to see you.

If you send a doctor anywhere near me, said Antoine, I shall kill him. But his illness persisted, and so did his friends, and one morning they brought a doctor – a brave doctor – to the restaurant. It was empty except for Antoine. He was seated at a table, a half-empty glass of calvados and a revolver in front of him, dead from a heart attack.

Is it true, or did he die peacefully in a clinic in Versailles? I know which ending I prefer, and I think Antoine would have preferred it too. It's better to die at home.

CONJURING
WITH
GRAPES

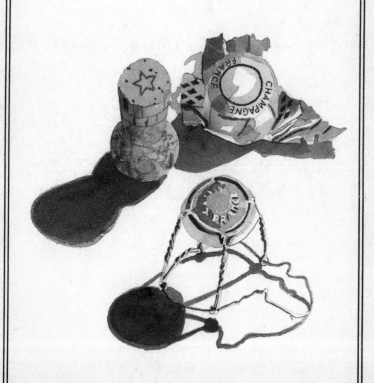

It is rare to be offered a choice of wines at breakfast, but I can recommend it, particularly on a brisk autumn morning in the heart of Champagne.

We were in the village of Bouzy, and had stopped at the house of Georges Vesselle for a little refreshment before attacking the serious business of the day. There was, of course, a glass or two of champagne to accompany the plates piled with *charcuterie* and the crisp *baguettes*. And then, with the ripe, pungent cheese, out came a few fat bottles of Bouzy, the only red wine produced in Champagne. This, I suppose, might seem excessive to those of you who confine yourselves each morning to a cup of black coffee and a bran muffin, but we had demanding work ahead of us, work that called for an alert palate and a well-lined stomach, and in these circumstances it is always wise to prepare yourself according to local customs.

My knowledge of champagne was skimpy, the odds and ends of information that any amateur will absorb over years of enthusiastic consumption. There are the grand houses and small producers, there are occasional vintage years, there are heavier and lighter tastes, larger or smaller bubbles – apart from that, champagne was to me a festive and romantic mystery, made by artists, no doubt, but I had only the vaguest idea of how they did it. Champagne, like perfect *pommes frites* or the love of a good woman, was just another blessing to accept gratefully.

This was about to change. After breakfast, we were driven to one of the most pleasantly named streets in the world – the Avenue de Champagne in Epernay – for a rendezvous with the nose and palate of André Bavaret.

Monsieur Bavaret has, each year, the responsibility for the taste and appearance of Perrier-Jouet – its delicacy and lightness, its subtlety, the finesse that gives it its special character. This must be consistent, year in and year out, despite capricious weather and the sometimes quirky behaviour of the vines, and therein lies the problem for anyone who attempts to compose a great champagne. And it is a composition, a blend; there is no such thing as a first-growth champagne.

First, Monsieur Bavaret explained, you must go shopping. He took us on a tour of the map on his wall which showed the villages and vineyards of Champagne. Altogether, his annual selection includes grapes from thirty-six scattered parcels of vines, and these are blended in proportions that change from year to year, according to variations in taste and quality. (Which is one reason why champagne can never be made by computer. There is no substitute for a gifted human palate.)

So we have our grapes. Now they must be assembled. We went through the office to the tasting room, where a regiment of plain green bottles and an army of glasses were arranged on a long white table. At each corner, I was relieved to see, was a waist-high *crachoir*; spitting was encouraged, which was just as well, because the wines were young and often tart. As we worked our way down the lines of glasses, my admiration grew for anyone who could make sense out of this confusion of tastes. There were, it's true, differences that were distinct enough even to my unprofessional taste buds. But how much of one and how little of another should go into the final blend? In many ways, it's like making perfume, with the added complication that it has to be a pleasure to swallow.

It was time for a conjuring trick. Monsieur Bavaret took something that resembled an oversized test tube, and poured into it varying amounts of the raw young wines that we had been tasting. He swirled them around in the test tube, added a final half glass from another anonymous green bottle, sniffed deeply, and nodded. This was a demonstration *cuvée*, to give us an idea of how blending can produce an instant smoothness from a combination of spiky flavours. The result was, magically, good enough to drink.

Thoughts of a second glass, just to make sure, had to be abandoned for a trip to the countryside. We were having lunch in a restored windmill at Verzenay, something light, we were told, to fortify us for the lessons of the afternoon.

Champagne scenery is like nothing else I've ever seen. It's

not dramatic – long, gentle hills for the most part, with the occasional sight of a tractor balancing on the skyline in the distance – but you will never find a better-kept stretch of country. Everywhere you look is neatness and order and thick, ruler-straight stripes of vines that seem to have been individually clipped to a uniform height. And, if you have been lucky enough to be invited to the windmill at Verzenay, you will see another characteristic, impressive and infinitely cheering sight: the man with the magnum.

He was waiting for us as we got out of the car. A ruddy face, topped by a dark blue cap, a long white apron, white gloves. His right arm was held close to his side and bent at the elbow, and his hand cradled the noble bottom of a magnum of Grand Cordon 1985 de Mumm. If there is a more welcome introduction to lunch than this, I have yet to see it.

As it turned out, the Grand Cordon was an aperitif, to be followed by other distinguished magnums: of Cramant de Mumm, of Perrier-Jouet Belle Epoque Rosé 1985, of Cordon Rouge de Mumm – all of them served with impeccable aim and rock-steady hand in a way that I could never attempt to copy. The expert does not hold the bottle by the neck or by the waist, but cups it from below, the thumb in the deep dimple of the base. The arm is extended, and the champagne is decanted with such smoothness and precision that the mousse stays just below the level of the rim of your glass. Bearing in mind the considerable weight of the magnum, the modest circumference of the champagne flute, the exuberance of the wine and the arm's-length delivery, the ritual seems fraught with potential catastrophe. Heaven known what would happen if I tried it.

It is a tribute to the stimulating qualities of really good champagne that by 2:30 we were not only awake, but clear-headed enough to look forward to the afternoon and our studies of the grape's progress, from bunches to bottles.

We began in the white-grape country of the Côtes des Blancs. The vines, which for long periods of the year are empty except for those few slow-moving and patient figures who check to see how nature is getting on, were now busy. The narrow green corridors were crowded with their autumn population of pickers. It was fine weather for the *vendange*, mile and dry, and the frosts of late spring had caused less havoc than predicted. This would be a good, plentiful year.

The baskets of grapes were passed up to collection points at the end of the vines, and ferried by truck or tractor to the village of Cramant and the waiting *pressoirs* of the house of Mumm. These presses, vast round wooden contraptions with slatted sides, are able to take tons of grapes at a single gulp. From above, very, very slowly, a giant wooden grill descends on them, bursts them, crushes them, and the juice runs off into subterranean vats.

Three times the grapes are subjected to this remorseless squeeze. Once, to extract the best of the juice, the *tête de cuvée*; a second time, for juice that can be used for blending; and finally, for the remains that will be distilled to make the local *eau de vie*, the *marc de Champagne* which they say grows hairs on your chest. Not a drop is wasted, and it is extraordinary to think that a single batch of grapes can be turned into two such different drinks, one delicate and light, the other – well, I happen to like *marc*, but you could never accuse it of being delicate.

We followed the route of the juice back to the fermentation casks, and here I should offer a word of warning. If anyone should ever suggest that you inhale the bouquet of champagne in its formative period, decline politely. I made the mistake of leaning over an open cask to take a connoisseur's sniff, and it felt like a noseful of needles. With watering eyes, I begged to go to a safer part of the production line, and we left the casks for an expedition into the bowels of the earth.

Beneath the two famous towns of Reims and Epernay are literally miles of cellars and passageways, some of them three or four storeys deep, and all of them filled with champagne. In these cool, dim caverns, the temperature never varies, and the bottles can doze in perfect conditions, mountain after dark green mountain of them, a champagne lover's foretaste of paradise.

We were in the Perrier-Jouet *caves*, not enormous by Champagne standards with a mere twelve million bottles, but sufficiently big to lose yourself in quite easily. The oldest *caves*, those immediately under the Perrier-Jouet offices, had been hacked out of the chalky earth by hand, and you can see the pick marks, now blackened by age, in the rough arches that lead from one *cave* to the next. Onward and downward we went, until we came to the angular ranks of tent-shaped wooden racks, each of them bristling with bottles.

The racks, or *pupitres*, as tall as a man, were invented in the nineteenth century to solve the problem of the sediment that forms in a bottle of champagne as a result of fermentation. The bottles are placed, neck first, in oval holes, at a steep angle that allows the sediment to slide up to the cork. To make sure this happens completely and evenly, the process needs, from time to time, a little assistance. The bottles have to be lifted gently, given a slight clockwise turn, and replaced. This is *remuage*, and despite experimenting with numerous mechanical methods, progress has yet to find a totally satisfactory replacement for the human hand. Cold and lonely work it must be, but a good *remueur* can deal with as many as 3000 bottles an hour.

After *remuage* comes *dégorgement*. The neck of the bottle is frozen, so that the sediment, trapped in ice, can be removed. The bottle is topped up, recorked, labelled, *et voilà*! What started as grapes in a muddy field has been transformed into nectar.

Should you drink it immediately, or lay it down for a year or two? (Or even longer, if it's a vintage champagne.) Experts disagree, as experts tend to do, and there are those who say that champagne kept too long will lose its sparkle and character. It depends, of course, on the quality of the wine, and I can personally vouch for the benefits of age that we enjoyed on our last night.

We'd been invited to dinner at the *hotel particulier* of Mumm in Reims. There was our old friend, the man with the magnum, and as the courses came and went, so did the '85 Cordon Rouge and the '85 Grand Cordon Rosé. For the finale, in a modestly unlabelled magnum, A Very Old Vintage was produced and served.

I held my glass up to the light and watched the whispers of tiny bubbles rising from the bottom. Whatever else the years might have done, they hadn't subdued the sparkle. They had, however, given the wine a very slightly toasted bouquet, the *pain grillé* nose of a truly venerable champagne. It tasted rich and delicate and dry, and it was thirty years old. There and then, I resolved never to drink cheap champagne again. Life is too short.

A taste of Peter Mayle's Provence is offered in this extract from *Toujours Provence*, sequel to the bestselling *A Year in Provence*, both of which are available from Pan Books.

No Spitting in
Châteauneuf-du-Pape

August in Provence is a time to lie low, to seek shade, to move slowly and to limit your excursions to very short distances. Lizards know best, and I should have known better.

It was in the high eighties by 9.30, and when I got into the car I immediately felt like a piece of chicken about to be *sautéed*. I looked at the map to find roads that would keep me away from the tourist traffic and heat-maddened truck drivers, and a bead of sweat dropped from my nose to score a direct hit on my destination – Châteauneuf-du-Pape, the small town with the big wine.

Months before, in the winter, I had met a man called Michel at a dinner to celebrate the engagement of two friends of ours. The first bottles of wine came. Toasts were proposed. But I noticed that while the rest of us were merely drinking, Michel was conducting a personal, very intense ritual.

He stared into his glass before picking it up, then cupped it in the palm of his hand and swirled it gently three or four times. Raising the glass to eye level, he peered at the traces of wine that his swirling had caused to trickle down the inner sides. His nose, with nostrils alert and flared, was presented to the wine and made a thorough investigation. Deep sniffing. One final swirl, and he took the first mouthful, but only on trial.

It obviously had to pass several tests before being allowed down the throat. Michel chewed it for a few reflective seconds. He pursed his lips and took a little air into his mouth and made discreet rinsing noises. Lifting his eyes to heaven, he flexed his cheeks in and out to encourage a free flow round tongue and molars and then, apparently satisfied with the wine's ability to withstand an oral assault course, he swallowed.

He noticed that I had been watching the performance, and grinned. '*Pas mal, pas mal.*' He took another, less elaborate swallow, and saluted the glass with raised eyebrows. 'It was a good year, '85.'

As I found out during dinner, Michel was a *négociant*, a professional wine drinker, a buyer of grapes and a seller of nectar. He specialized in the wines of the south, from Tavel *rosé* (the favourite wine, so he said, of Louis XIV) through the gold-tinged whites to the heavy, heady reds of Gigondas. But of all the wines in his extensive collection, his *merveille*, the one he would like to die drinking, was the Châteauneuf-du-Pape.

He described it as though he were talking about a woman. His hands caressed the air. Delicate kisses dusted his fingertips, and there was much talk of body and bouquet and *puissance*. It was not unknown, he said, for a Châteauneuf to reach fifteen degrees of alcoholic content. And these days, when Bordeaux seems to get thinner every year and the price of Burgundy is only possible for the Japanese, the wines of Châteauneuf are nothing less than bargains. I must come up to his *caves* and see for myself. He would arrange a *dégustation*.

The time that elapses in Provence between planning a rendezvous and keeping it can often stretch into months, and sometimes years, and so I wasn't expecting an immediate invitation. Winter turned to spring, spring turned to summer and summer melted into August, the most lethal month of the year to be toying with a fifteen-degree wine, and then Michel called.

'Tomorrow morning at eleven,' he said. 'In the *caves* at Châteauneuf. Eat plenty of bread at breakfast.'

I had done what he suggested and, as an extra precaution, taken a soup-spoonful of neat olive oil, which one of the local gourmets had told me was an excellent way to coat the stomach and cushion the system against repeated assault by young and powerful wines. In any case, I thought as I drove along the twisting, baked country roads, I wouldn't be swallowing much. I would do as the experts do, rinse and spit.

Châteauneuf came into view, trembling in the heat haze, just before eleven o'clock. It is a place entirely dedicated to wine. Seductive invitations are everywhere, on sunbleached peeling boards, on freshly painted posters, hand-lettered on monster bottles, fixed to the wall, propped at the side of vineyards, stuck on pillars at the end of driveways. *Dégustez! Dégustez!*

I drove through the gateway in the high stone wall that protects the Caves Bessac from the outside world, parked in the shade and unstuck myself from the car. I felt the sun come down on the top of my head like a close-fitting hat of hot air. In front of me was a long building, crenellated along the top, its façade blind except for huge double doors. A group of people, outlined against the black interior, were standing in the doorway, holding large bowls that glinted in the sun.

The *cave* felt almost cold, and the glass that Michel gave me was pleasantly cool in my hand. It was one of the biggest glasses I had ever seen, a crystal bucket on a stem, with a bulbous belly narrowing at the top to the circumference of a goldfish bowl. Michel said it could hold three-quarters of a bottle of wine.

My eyes adjusted to the gloom after the glare outside, and I began to realize that this was not a modest *cave*. Twenty-five thousand bottles would have been lost in the murk of one of the distant corners. In fact, there were no bottles to be seen, just boulevards of barrels – enormous barrels lying on their sides supported by waist-high platforms, their upper curves twelve or fifteen feet above the ground. Scrawled in chalk on the flat face of each barrel were descriptions of the contents, and for the first time in my life I was able to walk through a wine list: Côtes-du-Rhône-Villages, Lirac, Vacqueyras, Saint-Joseph, Crozes-Hermitage, Tavel, Gigondas – thousands of litres of each, arranged in vintages and dozing silently towards maturity.

'*Alors,*' said Michel, 'you can't walk around with an empty glass. What are you going to have?'

There was too much choice. I didn't know where to start. Would Michel guide me through the barrels? I could see that the others had something in their goldfish bowls; I'd have the same.

Michel nodded. That would be best, he said, because we only had two hours, and he didn't want to waste our time on the very young wines when there were so many treasures that were ready to drink. I was glad I'd had the olive oil.

Anything that qualified as a treasure was hardly spitting material. But two hours of swallowing would have me as supine as one of the barrels, and I asked if one was permitted to spit.

Michel waved his glass at a small drain that marked the entrance of the Boulevard Côtes-du-Rhône. *'Crachez si vous voulez, mais...'* It was clear that he thought it would be tragic to deny oneself the pleasure of the swallow, the bursting forth of flavours, the well-rounded finish and the profound satisfaction that comes from drinking a work of art.

The *maître de chai*, a wiry old man in a cotton jacket the colour of faded blue sky, appeared with a device that reminded me of a giant eye-dropper – three feet of glass tubing with a fist-sized rubber globe at one end. He aimed the nozzle and squeezed a generous measure of white wine into my glass, muttering a prayer as he squeezed: *'Hermitage '86, bouquet aux aromes de fleurs d'acacia. Sec, mais sans trop d'acidité.'*

I swirled and sniffed and rinsed and swallowed. Delicious. Michel was quite right. It would be a sin to consign this to the drain. With some relief, I saw that the others were tipping what they didn't drink into a large jug that stood on a nearby trestle table. Later, this would be transferred into a jar containing a *mère vinaigre*, and the result would be four-star vinegar.

Slowly, we worked our way down the boulevards. At each stop, the *maître de chai* climbed up his portable ladder to the top of the barrel, knocked out the bung and inserted his thirsty nozzle, returning down the ladder as carefully as if he were carrying a loaded weapon – which, as the tasting progressed, it began to resemble.

The first few shots had been confined to the whites, the

rosés and the lighter reds. But as we moved into the deeper gloom at the back of the *cave*, the wines too became darker. And heavier. And noticeably stronger. Each of them was served to the accompaniment of its own short but reverent litany. The red Hermitage, with its nose of violets, raspberries and mulberries, was a *vin viril*. The Côtes-du-Rhône *Grande Cuvée* was an elegant thoroughbred, fine and *étoffé*. I was impressed almost as much by the inventive vocabulary as by the wines themselves – fleshy, animal, muscular, well-built, voluptuous, sinewy – and the *maître* never repeated himself. I wondered whether he had been born with lyrical descriptive powers or whether he took a thesaurus to bed with him every night.

We finally arrived at Michel's *merveille*, the 1981 Châteauneuf-du-Pape. Although it would keep for many years to come, it was already a masterpiece, with its *robe profonde*, its hints of spice and truffle, its warmth, its balance – not to mention its alcoholic content, which was nudging fifteen degrees. I thought Michel was going to take a header into his glass. It's nice to see a man who loves his work.

With some reluctance, he put down his glass and looked at his watch. 'We must go,' he said. 'I'll get something to drink with lunch.' He went to an office at the front of the *cave*, and came out carrying a crate of a dozen bottles. He was followed by a colleague, carrying another dozen. Eight of us were going to lunch. How many would survive?

We left the *cave* and winced under the force of the sun. I had restrained myself to sips rather than mouthfuls; nevertheless, my head gave one sharp throb in warning as I walked to the car. Water. I must have water before even sniffing any more wine.

Michel thumped me on the back. 'There's nothing like a

dégustation to give you a thirst,' he said. 'Don't worry. We have a sufficiency.' Good grief.

The restaurant Michel had chosen was half an hour away, in the country outside Cavaillon. It was a *ferme auberge*, serving what he described as correct Provençal food in rustic surroundings. It was tucked away and hard to find, so I should stick closely to his car.

Easier said than done. So far as I know, there are no statistics to support my theory, but observation and heart-stopping personal experience have convinced me that a Frenchman with an empty stomach drives twice as fast as a Frenchman with a full stomach (which is already too fast for sanity and speed limits). And so it was with Michel. One minute he was there; the next he was a dust-smudged blur on the shimmering horizon, clipping the dry grass verges on the bends, booming through the narrow streets of villages in their midday coma, his gastronomic juices in overdrive. By the time we reached the restaurant, all pious thoughts of water were gone. I needed a drink.

The dining-room of the farm was cool and noisy. A large television set in the corner, ignored by the clientele, jabbered to itself. The other customers, mostly men, were darkened by the sun and dressed for outdoor work in old shirts and sleeveless vests, with the flattened hair and white foreheads that come from wearing a cap. A nondescript dog whiffled in the corner, nose twitching sleepily at the spicy smell of cooking meat coming from the kitchen. I realized that I was ravenous.

We were introduced to André, the *patron*, whose appearance, dark and full-bodied, fitted the description of some of the wines we'd been tasting. There were undertones of garlic, Gauloises and *pastis* present in his bouquet. He wore a loose shirt, short shorts, rubber sandals and an emphatic black moustache. He had a voice that transcended the hubbub of the room.

'*Eh, Michel! Qu'est-ce que c'est? Orangina? Coca-Cola?*' He started to unpack the crates of wine and reached in the back pocket of his shorts for a corkscrew. '*M'amour! Un seau, des glaçons, s'il te plaît.*'

His wife, sturdy and smiling, came out of the kitchen carrying a tray and unloaded it on the table: two ice buckets, plates of pink *saucisson* dotted with tiny peppercorns, a dish of vivid radishes and a deep bowl of thick *tapenade*, the olive and anchovy paste that is sometimes called the black butter of Provence. André was uncorking bottles like a machine, sniffing each cork as he drew it and arranging the bottles in a double line down the centre of the table. Michel explained that these were some of the wines we hadn't had time to try in the *cave*, young Côtes-du-Rhône for the most part, with half a dozen older and more serious reinforcements from Gigondas to help when the cheese arrived.

There is something about lunch in France that never fails to overcome any small reserves of will-power that I possess. I can sit down, resolved to be moderate, determined to eat and drink lightly, and be there three hours later, nursing my wine and still open to temptation. I don't think it's greed. I think it's the atmosphere generated by a roomful of people who are totally intent on eating and drinking. And while they do it, they talk about it; not about politics or sport or business, but about what is on the plate and in the glass. Sauces are compared, recipes argued over, past meals remembered and future meals planned. The world and its problems can be dealt with later on, but for the moment, *la bouffe* takes priority and contentment hangs in the air. I find it irresistible.

We eased into lunch like athletes limbering up. A radish, its top split open to hold a sliver of almost white butter and flecked with a pinch of coarse salt; a slice of *saucisson*, prickly with pepper on the tongue; rounds of toast made from yesterday's bread, shining with *tapenade*. Cool pink and white wines. Michel leaned across the table. 'No spitting.'

The *patron*, who was nipping away at a glass of red in between his duties, presented the first course with as much ceremony as a man in shorts and rubber sandals can muster, placing a deep *terrine*, its sides burnt almost black, on the table. He stuck an old kitchen knife into the *pâté*, then came back with a tall glass pot of *cornichons* and a dish of onion jam. '*Voilà, mes enfants. Bon appétit.*'

The wine changed colour as Michel dealt out his young reds, and the *terrine* was passed around the table for second slices. André came over from his card game to refill his glass. '*Ça va? Ça vous plaît?*' I told him how much I liked his onion jam. He told me to save some room for the next course, which was – he kissed his fingertips loudly – a triumph, *alouettes sans tête*, prepared specially for us by the hands of his adorable Monique.

Despite the rather grisly name (literally, larks without heads), it is a dish made from thin slices of beef rolled around slivers of salt pork, seasoned with chopped garlic and parsley, bathed in olive oil, dry white wine, stock and tomato *coulis* and served neatly trussed with kitchen twine. It looks nothing like a lark – more like an opulent sausage – but some creative Provençal cook must have thought that larks sounded more appetizing than rolled beef, and the name has survived.

Monique brought in the *alouettes*, which André said he had shot that morning. He was a man who found it difficult to make a joke without delivering the punch line physically, and the nudge he delivered with his forearm almost knocked me into a vast tub of *ratatouille*.

The headless larks were hot and humming with garlic, and Michel decided that they deserved a more solid wine. The Gigondas was promoted from the cheese course, and the collection of dead bottles at the end of the table was by now well into double figures. I asked Michel if he had any plans to work in the afternoon. He looked surprised. 'I *am* working,' he said. 'This is how I like to sell wine. Have another glass.'

Salad came, and then a basketwork tray of cheeses – fat white discs of fresh goat cheese, some mild Cantal and a wheel of creamy St Nectaire from the Auvergne. This inspired André, now installed at the head of the table, to produce another joke. There was this little boy in the Auvergne who was asked which he liked best, his mother or his father. The little boy thought for a moment. 'I like bacon best,' he said. André heaved with laughter. I was relieved to be out of nudging distance.

Scoops of sorbet were offered, and an apple tart, sleek with glaze, but I was defeated. When André saw me shake my head, he bellowed down the table, 'You must eat. You need your strength. We're going to have a game of *boules*.'

After coffee, he led us outside to show us the goats that he kept in a pen at the side of the restaurant. They were huddled in the shade of an outbuilding, and I envied them; they weren't being asked to play *boules* under a sun which was drilling lasers into the top of my head. It was no good. My eyes were aching from the glare and my stomach wanted desperately to lie down and digest in peace. I made my excuses, found a patch of grass under a plane tree and lowered my lunch to the ground.

André woke me some time after six and asked if I was staying for dinner. There were *pieds et paquets*, he said, and by some happy chance two or three bottles of the Gigondas had survived. With some difficulty, I escaped and drove home.

My wife had spent a sensible day in the shade and by the pool. She looked at me, a rumpled apparition, and asked if I had enjoyed myself.

'I hope they gave you something to eat,' she said.